Communicate with
Emotional Intelligence

Communicators is an imprint of How To Books.
For further details please send for a free copy of the latest catalogue
3 Newtec Place, Magdalen Road, Oxford OX4 1RE United Kingdom

Communicate
with Emotional
Intelligence

John Eaton and Roy Johnson

communicators

Published by How To Books Ltd,
3 Newtec Place, Magdalen Road,
Oxford OX4 1RE. United Kingdom.
Tel: (01865) 793806. Fax: (01865) 248780
email: info@howtobooks.co.uk
http://www.howtobooks.co.uk

First edition 2001

British Library Cataloguing in Publication Data.
A catalogue record for this book is available from the British Library.

Edited by Francesca Mitchell
Cover design by Baseline Arts Ltd, Oxford

Produced for How To Books by Deer Park Productions
Typeset and design by Baseline Arts Ltd, Oxford
Printed and bound by Bell & Bain Ltd, Glasgow

NOTE: The material contained in this book is set out in good faith for general
guidance and no liability can be accepted for loss or expense incurred as a result
of relying in particular circumstances on statements made in this book. Laws
and regulations are complex and liable to change, and readers should check the
current position with the relevant authorities before making personal
arrangements.

Communicators is an imprint of How To Books.

Contents

Preface 7

1 What is Emotional Intelligence? 11

Understand how emotional intelligence works through fascinating research in this area. Find out how emotional intelligence is crucial to your career success.

2 Self-Management 32

How to gain mastery over your emotions, make good decisions, and build positive states that enable you to work at your best.

3 Reading Others Well 53

Develop your 'social radar' by noticing subtle clues and using empathy to anticipate others' reactions to what you have to say.

4 Persuasive Communication 74

Build influential messages by linking what you say to your audience's core values. Win agreement with your proposals by rehearsing your points and structuring them logically.

5 Managing Conflict 96

Get rid of fear and anger by understanding and letting go. Substitute cool reason for runaway emotions and resolve conflicts through win-win thinking.

6 Widening Your Influence 118

Advice on everything from networking to playing politics, from motivating others to creating an impact on key decision-makers.

Preface

Welcome to the world of emotional intelligence – one of the fastest growing fields in business, education and psychology today.

Our purpose in writing this book is to assist you in harnessing the power of emotion to the way you speak to and relate to others. This will undoubtedly raise your powers of persuasion and self-belief. It will also enable you to forge relationships which will help you in your personal and professional life. The evidence suggests that career success is closely related to the skills we describe in this book.

Like most readers we were familiar with emotional intelligence long before we heard of the label. All the examples of emotionally intelligent communication we provide in this book are in fact taken from real-life. We are sure that you will be able to come up with many examples of your own. In fact the more you are able to do this the more impact this book is likely to have on you. The point is that some people are emotionally very clever while others are just not very good at it. We aim to help you to learn from the former and to watch out for the latter.

The basis of all emotional intelligence is simple: noticing emotions in yourself and others, and using them to make good decisions. Because this is a very practical thing to do we ask you to follow the activities we provide in the book and to practise the skills of emotional intelligence for yourself. While we provide the railway track the engine of emotion and action must be provided by you, the reader.

This is a book for reading in sequence and for dipping in to. The first three chapters are best read in sequence, as they describe the basics of emotional intelligence. The last three chapters delve more into applications and uses.

This book was written with heart and we hope that it speaks to yours. At bottom we believe that success in any area of life comes from knowing yourself well, learning to get along with others, acting with passion, cultivating peace and serenity, and pursuing worthwhile goals. This book is a small contribution to those ideals.

John Eaton and Roy Johnson

To Yvonne and Jane – our emotionally intelligent guides. With love.

Chapter 1

What is Emotional Intelligence?

In this Chapter:

- **distinguishing emotional cleverness from other kinds of intelligence**
- **how successful people use emotional intelligence**
- **developing emotional intelligence by paying attention to our emotions and what they tell us to do**
- **understanding and using the skills of emotional intelligence.**

Emotional intelligence is the ability to inform our decisions with an understanding of our own and others' emotions so that we can take productive action. Research shows that career success depends crucially on this skill. Emotionally intelligent people rise to the top in business because they are self-motivated and self-confident. They are not at the mercy of out-of-control emotions. They may be disappointed by setbacks, but they recover from them quickly. Mastery of their inner world is not enough, however. Emotionally intelligent people also turn sensitivity to their own feelings outwards. Their empathy for others makes them perceptive in working with others and, thus, influential. They, like James in the example below, are excellent at forging alliances with people that lead to mutually beneficial outcomes.

James and Peter: emotional contrasts

James is a talented sales manager predicted to reach the top in the company he works for.

> James's thoughts on reorganizing direct sales catch the interest of the sales director, who asks James to present his ideas to the Board. Before he does so, James sounds out other departments likely to be affected by his proposals if they are accepted. He adapts his ideas to accommodate the vested interests involved, without sacrificing his overall goal. Come the presentation, he is surprised by the unexpected criticism of the finance director, who, unknown to James, has initiated a cost-cutting exercise in response to a hole in the accounts that has only just come to light. James is upset but keeps his cool. He clarifies the finance director's objections and draws out the conditions under which his ideas might be accepted in the current circumstances and in more favourable future conditions. Reflecting on the meeting later, he sees his failure to convince the Board as bad luck and sets to work on a proposal for a pilot scheme that would test his ideas without undue cost.

Peter is also an up and coming manager. He is bright, ambitious and full of ideas for improving the efficiency and effectiveness of his company's product distribution.

> Peter's director asks him to present his ideas at a Board meeting. He does so with élan and his enthusiasm is plain to all present.
> Unfortunately, the sales and marketing director and the finance director savage his ideas. His proposals are seen to be costly and out of tune with a new marketing strategy. Peter is shell-shocked and walks out of the meeting in a daze. As he dwells on his treatment, he becomes increasingly resentful and decides that the company has no room for people with new ideas. He starts to play politics and tries to manoeuvre against the Board members whom he sees as out to 'get' him. Very soon he becomes isolated and is left out of important decisions. When, a little while later, he is turned down for an important promotion, he resigns in disgust. His time at the company has ended in failure.

Peter, unlike James, allows his emotions to rule him. He is also blind to the intentions of others. Instead of checking things out he jumps to emotionally destructive conclusions that leave him resentful. Yet, unable to detach himself from these assumptions, he ends in a state of isolation. He would do better to channel his enthusiasm into productive action that attracts the support of others instead of involving him in futile conflict. In this book we aim to help you to avoid the fate of Peter and develop the skills that James possesses.

The origins of emotional intelligence

'Emotional Intelligence' is a term made popular by Daniel Goleman in his best-selling books *Emotional Intelligence* (1996) and *Working With Emotional Intelligence* (1998). Research into this topic has a long history. Long before Goleman's work, psychologists were studying 'social intelligence' – the ability to get along well with others – and it was concluded in the 1940s that leaders were often warm people with a gift for developing relationships based on mutual trust and respect. Later on, Howard Gardner showed that there was more to intelligence than just IQ – that in addition to verbal and mathematical cleverness there was kinaesthetic, spatial and musical intelligence as well as interpersonal and intrapersonal skill. 'Intrapersonal' skill refers to the ability to relate well to others, while 'intrapersonal' skill means having a good understanding of your own inner world of thoughts and feelings. Both of these are linked to emotional intelligence, as we shall see later.

Over the past ten years much psychological research has been carried out in the field of emotional intelligence (i.e. interpersonal and intrapersonal intelligence). Indeed Goleman's books contain not just his own ideas, but summaries and discussions of many other studies. So far, most of the research has been carried out in education (helping children to learn with emotionally intelligent teaching), personality (what distinguishes emotionally intelligent people from others) and business (characteristics of high-performing managers and teams). In this book we focus on communication and how to improve it.

The different kinds of intelligence

The Oxford Dictionary defines intelligence as 'the intellect; the understanding', and defines the intellect in particular as 'the faculty of reasoning, knowing, and thinking, as distinct from feeling'. Thus, we have a narrow definition of intelligence: the sort you can measure with IQ tests and with academic exam results. For a long time, in the earlier part of this century, this was the only form of intelligence studied by most psychologists.

In the 1980s, Howard Gardner broadened the subject when he published his theory of multiple intelligences, in which he argued that success in life was not just dependent on IQ. He showed that there were seven different types of intelligence:

◆ **Linguistic.** The ability to use and comprehend language. Those gifted here may be writers, speakers, scholars or good listeners.
◆ **Logical.** The ability to solve logical and mathematical problems. Produces mathematicians, philosophers, statisticians, accountants, logicians and scientists.
◆ **Spatial.** The ability to work with visual and spatial forms and patterns. Excellent for pilots, engineers, painters, sculptors, and navigators. Also gives the ability to 'read' ball games and chessboards as well as recognize faces.

◆ **Musical.** Includes the ability to appreciate music as well as compose, play, conduct or sing it.

◆ **Kinaesthetic.** The intelligent and flexible use of one's body. Useful for athletes, actors, dancers, surgeons and artists.

◆ **Interpersonal.** The ability to relate well to others by understanding their inner thoughts and feelings, and responding to their moods and intentions. Traditionally this skill has been important to salespeople, teachers, psychotherapists and managers of people.

◆ **Intrapersonal.** The ability to monitor one's own subtle thoughts, feelings, sensations and moods, and to be guided by them in making decisions. Includes the ability to get in touch with personal desires, dreams, hopes and values.

Instances of people gifted in one intelligence but 'stupid' in others are numerous. To take examples from the cinema: there is the great concert pianist prone to sudden rages (lacking intrapersonal intelligence); the champion athlete who is tongue-tied (lacking linguistic intelligence); and the university professor who dances like an elephant (lacking kinaesthetic intelligence). In business similar caricatures abound.

The tyrannical boss

She is direct, blunt and determined. She likes to have her own way. She treads on others' feelings with ruthless disregard. Originally a lawyer, she has fought her way to the top through her brilliance in mastering a brief. Dealing with complex legal affairs she can get straight to the heart of the matter and summarize it instantly. Whether in court, in the boardroom, or when dealing with clients she dominates the discussion with her grasp of the facts and her ability to argue a case. Her reports and presentations are notable for their ability to marshal the facts. However, she has few allies and has made many enemies. Few of her staff are close to her and none dares to answer her back. With a string of broken relationships behind her she lives alone.

'Mr Spock'

He is the Financial Controller. He has been with the company for many years and has acquired knowledge of every aspect of its finances, from its quarterly profit figures to the cost of an office chair. He can analyze a cash flow forecast at a glance and notice a single figure out of place. At meetings he contributes to discussions with a voice like a 'speak-your-weight' machine. He likes to give two alternatives to every decision: the 'right' one, which he supports with a stream of figures and analysis, and the 'irrational' one. He abhors risk and adventure and rarely gets excited about the company's prospects. He lives for his work and has no interests outside it. On the rare occasions he speaks about his personal life, he gives the impression that it is as dull as his working one.

The office flirt

He is the life and soul of the party. He is popular and funny, and most people find him utterly charming. He works in Customer Relations and is on excellent terms with all the company's important clients. Indeed, many of them, when they call for a meeting, ask for him by name. Thus he is always dashing off to business lunches, cocktail parties and dinner events. He has had a string of affairs with other employees and is also the company gossip. He likes nothing better than to be surrounded by a crowd listening to his every word in the pub after office hours. He rarely stays in one job for long because, although popular, he is a bad decision-maker. In his last job he negotiated a business deal that lost the company tens of thousands of pounds – and all because he hadn't the heart to say no to a client he liked. He rarely stops to think about the business he is in and cannot put a proposal together to save his life. He has to get his PA to analyze his figures, make sense of his ideas, and make decisions.

Which dimensions of intelligence do you think are shown by these characters? What forms of intelligence are they lacking?

Answers

The tyrannical boss
Possesses linguistic intelligence but deficient in
interpersonal skills.

'Mr Spock'
Possesses logical intelligence but deficient in intrapersonal
intelligence.

The office flirt
Possesses interpersonal intelligence but lacks foresight and
staying power – the ability to regulate his emotions
intelligently.

Why conventional intelligence is not enough

In assessing people for job vacancies, tests tend to
overvalue factors such as academic achievement, technical
training and verbal reasoning. The ability to think clearly
and logically and to solve problems is important in
business, as is the ability to write, speak and
communicate well. In some fields the gift of spatial
intelligence is also a must. However, for long-term career
success it is also important to possess interpersonal and
intrapersonal skill. The reason for this is that seniority
requires a flair for working with others and managing
them. Psychological research shows that having a high IQ
may play only a 10% part in predicting eventual career
success. Too often, intellectually gifted people can be
sidelined if they do not also have the emotional
intelligence to make alliances, deal with conflict,

overcome crises, and retain poise and balance. The good news is that, with some exceptions, most people can learn to develop these skills.

Emotionally intelligent people use both *intrapersonal* and *interpersonal* skills together. Interpersonal intelligence is the ability to understand and work co-operatively with others. It is based on openness and a willingness to explore the interests of others. Intrapersonal intelligence, on the other hand, looks inwards. It cultivates self-understanding as a basis for effective action. In fact, it is unlikely that people could have one without the other. For example, learning to recognize one's own moods is key to recognizing mood changes in others. Similarly, practising self-restraint is fundamental to the ability to maintain good relationships. Emotional intelligence, therefore, is the ability to recognize emotions in oneself and others and to make productive decisions based on this information.

Exercise

Which of these are examples of an emotionally intelligent decision?

1. A supervisor realizes that one of her team-members is repeatedly coming in late looking stressed. She decides it is more tactful to ignore the lateness and wait for things to right themselves, as it is a personal matter for the employee.

2. A customer relations manager finds that one particular buyer is highly irritating to deal with. The buyer commonly cancels appointments, treats him in an off-

hand way, and frequently changes her mind about orders. He decides to tackle her about it and to ask if there is anything he can do to improve their relationship.

3. A business coach is asked to work with a manager who has been given three months to improve his performance or face dismissal. At their first meeting, the manager is apathetic and spends most of his time complaining about the unfairness of his employers. The business coach gathers the facts from him, agrees that things might look unfair, and asks what most useful course of action is open to him.

4. A sales manager gives a disastrous presentation. It is the first one she has ever done, and she dries up in front of the audience. Several people leave early and she has to bring the whole thing to an early conclusion. She decides that she is not cut out for presentations and that it is wiser to leave them to those with talent for them.

Answers
Numbers 2 and 3 are examples of emotionally intelligent decisions.

How emotions drive us to act

The Latin root of the word 'emotion' is *motere* meaning 'to move'. So emotions drive us to act. Some researchers claim to have identified the basic emotions that are independent of our conscious mind – feelings like fear, anger, surprise, disgust and affection. More complex emotions like guilt, hope and sympathy are a result of a complex interaction in the brain between the thinking centres and the thalamus. Our emotions affect us profoundly and, being mostly outside our conscious control, can run away with us. We do not, however, need to be their slaves. Mindfulness, reflection and conscious control allow us to regulate our emotions, link them to our cherished goals, and act in more productive ways.

Without emotions life would appear to us as a stream of unconnected events – just one damn thing after another. Emotions are crucial in motivating us to make choices and in bestowing meaning and purpose on what we do. They also make it possible for us to interact with other people and, in turn, to become the sort of people that others want to be with. Let's look at the example of Elliott – a real-life victim of brain injury.

How Elliott lost his capacity for emotional intelligence

An operation to remove a tumour from Elliott's brain had caused a loss of healthy tissue, which meant the connections between the thinking centres and the emotional brain had been severed. When you and I are shown photographs of a gory accident, we are disturbed. Our pulse rate and blood pressure increase, and stress hormones enter the blood stream. By contrast, Elliott experienced no such response. To him the photographs were equivalent to looking at a filing cabinet. His conventional intelligence was unimpaired and he could continue to do sums and understand a complex chapter in a book. However, Elliott found it difficult to make even the simplest decisions, like getting up in the morning or making an appointment. His ability to earn a living was seriously impaired because he had not the slightest interest in things that happened to him, even when these were disastrous. He was unable to distinguish between a good choice and a bad one. He saw no particular reason to do a job well, although he could understand how it should be done. Nor did he have the emotional staying power to see a task right through to the end. He lost a series of contracts and was reduced to bankruptcy before he sought help for his difficulties.

Elliott's problem was caused by the severance of neuronal connections between the frontal cortex, the seat of consciousness, and the limbic system – the area of the brain in which emotions are generated. The frontal cortex could register an external stimulus, like the photographs, but no messages were ever sent on from there to the emotional brain, leaving him unable to evaluate the significance of what was happening.

The emotional alarm system

We, unlike Elliott, experience a continuous emotional traffic in which external events are picked up visually and aurally and information is registered in the brain in the frontal lobes as well as in the limbic system and the amygdala. The response of the amygdala is particularly fast. It needs to be as it prompts our fight or flight response, which is vital to our survival. When we are woken by a noise in the house at night, immediately our senses are heightened, prompted by the response of the amygdala. Fortunately, the conscious mind processes the information too, enabling us to think through the possible causes, put it down to the cat and go back to sleep.

More slowly than this, the limbic system sends a stream of messages through the nervous system that are experienced as changes in the gut, the circulation of the blood, the muscles, heart and lungs. The raw material of emotion enables us to connect to our experiences and bestow a value on them: good, bad, indifferent, frightening, joyful or sympathetic. In this way we are motivated to act on them (or, in some cases, ignore them). With too little emotion, we lose staying power and the ability to evaluate what is best for us and others. With too much, we lose our sense of judgement and self-control.

Developing emotional intelligence

Understanding our emotions and those of others, and dealing constructively with them, can help us in all kinds of ways.

Miranda's emotional intelligence contributes to her success

Miranda runs her own successful training business and is a caring mother of her two teenage children. Sometimes the demands of these arenas of her life clash. When they do, she negotiates with her husband and children or with her partners, employees and customers. Most of the time she manages to forge win-win agreements. Sometimes this is not possible and she accepts these situations calmly while doing her best to maintain the relationship. Her colleagues respect her very much as there is not one of them who has not experienced her generosity and concern. As a result she has positive emotional bank balances with nearly all of them. There is a sense of fun in her company. Frequent celebrations entertain company staff, customers and associates and help to forge loyal relationships. The company's training is highly regarded and, as a consequence, earns high fees. Part of the reason for this is that Miranda and her colleagues genuinely want to make a difference and are inspired by strong social ideals.

It has not always been plain sailing. In its early days, Miranda's business was close to failure. It was depressing but she retained her ability to act productively and keep

> going. Her wide network of contacts
> brought forth a backer ready to provide
> funds until the difficulty had been
> weathered. She also took advice and
> appointed an experienced manager to install
> strong financial controls. Her business is well
> placed now. Sometimes she feels as if it is
> all too much, but these feelings are short-
> lived and she is buoyed by her inherent
> sense of optimism. She is profoundly
> intelligent at the emotional level.

Emotional intelligence requires practice. This book can show you how it is done but cannot give it to you. Learning to read your own emotional responses, and to respond fruitfully to those of others, takes time. Moreover, some of these lessons can be uncomfortable, or just sheer hard work. Emotional intelligence requires emotional honesty: the capacity to face up to our mistakes and inadequacies. This book can provide you with ideas but not experiences; these must come from you, the reader. We have made this book as interactive as possible by providing you with exercises, questions and activities. Engaging with these will enable emotional intelligence to come alive in you.

We can improve our emotional intelligence by developing the skills shown by emotionally intelligent people. Not all emotionally intelligent people have the same skills. In the examples given earlier in this chapter:

- The customer relations manager has two skills: reading relationships well and holding an assertive conversation.
- The business coach possesses the skill of active listening and motivating the client to focus on action.
- The sales manager lacks the ability to recover from emotional setbacks, although she might possess the skill of understanding her limitations.
- The supervisor may have the skill of tact but lacks empathy – the ability to put oneself in others' shoes and understand them.

Miranda (the owner of the training business) shows the major skills of emotional intelligence, including:

- **Self-awareness**
  With this, you understand your own emotions and recognize them as they occur. Your emotional responses guide you in different situations. You recognize your limitations and make the most of your strengths.

- **Self-confidence**
  Based on a realistic awareness of their limitations, confident people know when to trust in their own decisions and when to defer to others. Making the most of their strengths, confident people continually engage in new challenges that expand personal potential.

◆ **Self-regulation**
This ability enables you to stay focused on your goals and delay gratification until they are accomplished. You recover from setbacks quickly and see goals through to the end. Destructive emotional responses are put aside in favour of ones more likely to achieve the goal. You motivate yourself by staying in touch with your most important aspirations.

◆ **Motivation**
This ability enables you to inspire others by focusing on their needs, preferences, values, goals and personal strengths.

◆ **Empathy**
With empathy, you attune to the needs, values, wishes and perspectives of others. You sense others' feelings and thoughts by actively placing yourself in their position.

◆ **Social acumen**
Reading situations quickly and well, both verbally and non-verbally, enables you to adapt to the intentions of those with whom you have a relationship. Your sensitivity to group dynamics enables you to identify who in the group is most influential and to align with the cultural style of others.

◆ **Persuasiveness**
Emotionally intelligent people are adept at reading the intentions and wishes of others and creating mutually satisfactory outcomes. They develop the habit of

win/win thinking and look for ways in which personal goals can be aligned with those of others.

◆ **Conflict management**
With this ability you anticipate conflict before it occurs and divert attention to more productive courses of action. If conflict develops, you resolve it by focusing the attention of the parties involved on actions that are in their best interests.

Using interpersonal and intrapersonal strengths

Perhaps the best way to develop *interpersonal* skill is to observe people who are gifted in this area. Notice how such people speak and look at others. Listen to their words and the moves through which they collaborate with others.

Intrapersonal skill involves listening well, noticing responses, using win/win thinking, resolving conflict, and maintaining poise. It is most important to listen to your own emotions and reactions. Recognize what motivates you and link your most important needs and values to your goals. Foster your ability to master adversity by recalling times in your life when you were able to do so: when you dealt with conflicts, setbacks and disappointments. What did you do then that worked well? Make a note of your answers and be ready to deploy those skills again.

Such skills are described in this book. In developing them, you too will become an emotionally intelligent communicator. By practising the exercises you will give yourself the opportunity to learn and grow. In doing this you will be more successful in:

◆ negotiation
◆ coaching
◆ presentations
◆ sales
◆ performance reviews
◆ holding meetings
◆ interviewing
◆ leadership
◆ customer relations
◆ team-building.

In summary ...

◆ 'Emotional intelligence' refers to our ability to inform our decisions with an understanding of our own and others' emotions in order to act productively.

◆ Emotional intelligence is one type of intelligence amongst many others. It means the ability to manage our own emotions (intrapersonal intelligence) and the ability to interact well with others (interpersonal intelligence).

◆ Emotional intelligence is crucial to long-term success in business.

◆ Emotions act as warning signals when there is trouble ahead, motivate us to overcome adversity, and enable us to make good decisions.

◆ The key skills that go with emotional intelligence include: reading people well, acting with poise and confidence, motivating and persuading others, empathy, decision-making, and managing conflict.

Chapter 2

Self-Management

In this Chapter:

- **building self-confidence and positive thinking**
- **how to master your own emotions**
- **how gut reactions help you to make good decisions**
- **recalling emotionally positive states to help you work at your best**
- **staying focused and calm as you communicate with others.**

The old song tells us that it is not what you do but the way that you do it that gets results. Presenters fail to inspire us, even though they are familiar with their subject, if they don't engage our interest. Much of a presenter's appeal is bound up with non-verbal communication, rather than content. Non-verbal communication – body language and voice quality – is a vital component of credibility in face-to-face interaction. But the journey starts on the inside.

Credible communicators are self-confident; they know what they want and think positively. They use their gut feelings as a guide to decisions. They know when to commit to something and what to avoid. An ounce of commitment is worth more to them than a ton of vague wishes. Setbacks occur, of course. Emotionally intelligent communicators, however, retain credibility by bouncing back quickly. Their self-belief shows in their commitment over the long term. They get results because they say what they have to say convincingly.

Knowing what you want

In a well known quote from Lewis Carroll's *Alice in Wonderland*, Alice asks the Cheshire cat the way she should go from here. In reply, the cat asks Alice where she wants to go, but Alice says that she doesn't really care. The wise Cat tells her that in that case it doesn't matter which way she goes. This applies equally in communication. Without a goal communicators cannot plan their best route or know whether they are on or off track.

The most effective goals live in the mind as a vivid projection of a desired future. The best athletes picture themselves bursting through the tape in first place, and championship-winning skiers run through an event in their mind's eye in great detail before they race. Like good athletes, good communicators create a vivid imagine of the outcome of their communication. It inspires them and enthuses others.

Exercise

Think about an important interaction you face – a meeting, a presentation or a negotiation – and develop a goal for it by following the steps below.

◆ Make sure the goal is **positive** – what you want from the interaction rather than what you do not want.

◆ **Imagine** achieving your outcome for the meeting: what you will see, hear and feel afterwards.

◆ Focus on what is in your **control**, namely your own behaviour. Which actions are most likely to secure your outcome?

◆ Identify the personal **strengths** that will support you in achieving your goal – skills, experiences, talents, support from others. Which ones will you use?

◆ Bring the goal to life by **stepping into the future** as if you had already achieved it. Then look back from your future to the present and identify the first, important step you took along the way. Remember – the first step starts today!

Thinking positively

Faced with failure, optimists review events that led to the failure to find out what they can learn from it. They see where bad luck played its part and how others contributed to the result. They do not blame themselves but focus on what can be learned from the experience. Optimists see success as a comment on themselves. This boost to their self-esteem gives them the self-confidence to take on bigger challenges. Pessimists have more or less the reverse strategy. They see failure as 'proof' that they are helpless. This reduces their self-esteem, making them more cautious and less confident. They put success down to good luck or to the contribution of others, rather than to their own efforts. They fail to learn from their mistakes, writing them off to the curse of 'bad luck'.

From failure to eventual success: Abraham Lincoln

Abraham Lincoln, like many other great leaders, is a good example. He was born in a poor area of Kentucky in 1809 and received little education. His family moved to Indiana and for a time lived in a shack with only three walls. He lost his mother at the age of nine. From the age of 22 he spent six years drifting through menial jobs. He took this as a comment on the need to learn a profession and so he studied law in his spare time. His practice did not thrive and so he went into politics. He failed three times before sheer persistence led to his election to the state legislature. His legal practice eventually began to prosper and he found a business partner with whom he established a life-long relationship of trust and mutual support. However, his criticism of the Mexican war led to his being thrown out of office as a Congressman in 1849.

Lincoln then withdrew from politics and he, and most others, thought his career was over. But he spent the next six years in private life developing a vision of a United States free from slavery, which drew many supporters. His next attempt to fight an election – to the Senate as an anti-slavery campaigner – also failed, but his brilliant speeches added to his reputation. Even so, his nomination as a

Presidential candidate only occurred because
the Republican party could not agree and he
was the compromise candidate. He was finally
elected president of the USA in 1860.
Throughout his career, he was supported by his
strong self-belief, his persistence and
adaptability, and his ability to reflect on his
setbacks and draw lessons from them. He was
also gifted with the ability to inspire loyalty and
affection in those who worked closely with him.

Learning from success and failure

Think positively about your chances of success and, like
Lincoln, learn how to make the most of your talents.
When things go well, then do more of the things that
helped you to make them a success. Lincoln, for
example, eventually achieved success as a lawyer when he
discovered that he was a good commercial lawyer –
handling property claims relating to railroad companies.
In his legal practice, however, he wisely allowed his
partner to handle the work he was not suited to. So long
as Lincoln stuck to his strengths he was successful. He
also learned to make alliances with people who had gifts
he did not possess.

When a setback happens, look dispassionately at what went
wrong and consider it as valuable information that will help
you to improve for the future. If no lessons seem to be
available, then use the opportunity to stand back from
failure and assess your values and priorities. It would seem
that Lincoln had three strategies for dealing with failures.

The first was to persevere until success came along. The second was to reflect on what experience had taught him so far – and then to take remedial action; the third was to withdraw altogether and to reassess his involvement. This last step often led to some life-changing decisions, as when he first decided to study law and also, when late in life, he became a national anti-slavery campaigner.

Cultivating optimism

Like Lincoln, cultivate an optimist's frame of mind. Give yourself time to review your meetings, interviews and presentations. Learn from what worked and what did not work. Ask yourself how you could improve in the future. Pat yourself on the back for successes. Use positive experiences that you have had in the past to boost your confidence now and in the future. Think of meetings in which you made a telling contribution, coaching sessions that helped somebody, presentations that inspired people, conversations in which you swayed opinion. If you cannot think of any successful communications then think of successes in sport, social life or home life. These experiences are gold dust; they can transform your emotional state. Choose a past success that makes you feel self-confident before you walk into a meeting, presentation or interview. Think of occasions in your past when you have been relaxed and creative; it will put you in the right frame of mind for successful communication.

Finally, think carefully about your strengths and learn to make the most of them. Take, for example, the project manager who was asked to make a presentation to a senior management team. Her anxiety was understandable. She had never made a formal presentation, let alone to seniors like this. To lessen her nervousness she decided to rely on her acknowledged ability to teach people how to use computer applications. She used a computer in her presentation. This put her on familiar ground and gave her a greater sense of self-confidence.

Exercise

◆ Make a list of the strengths you identified in the last exercise. Now add all the other strengths you can think of from other areas of your life – work, home and personal life. Ask people who know you well to offer their opinion on your strengths. List those, too.

◆ Now identify your long-term goals, specifying at least one each for your career, your personal interests, and your relationships. Be specific about the goals you select.

◆ Now look at your list of strengths. Which ones can you use to achieve your goals? Make a note of how you will use them, what you will do, and when.

Listening to your gut feelings

Your emotions are a crucial guide to important decisions. Logic is not enough. It can tell you the pros and cons but your decision will ultimately be based on gut reactions. Remember the case of Elliott, described in Chapter 1; he made mistakes with the simplest of decisions because he had no inner feelings to guide him.

Use your intuition

The best decisions are informed by intuition as well as rational analysis. When managers recruit new team members, the qualifications and experience of candidates can be specified. But they are also judging the candidate's talent, and how they fit with the team and the company culture. Often, they will rely on their 'feel' for the person in front of them, using this intuitive sense as a rough-and-ready guide to suitability. Likewise, when salespeople decide on a new marketing campaign, only certain factors can be specified: costs, brands, market sectors, possible benefits. The rest comes from intuitive knowledge based on experience and a feel for the way the market is going.

The element of risk

There is always an element of risk to each decision you make. Often the choices are evenly balanced and there is no sure way of knowing which is the right one. To some extent the risk can be measured but, in the end, it comes down to the manager's gut feeling about whether the risk is likely to pay off given the present state of the market. Of course, gut feelings can be wrong, but often this is because we don't listen to them well enough.

Your internal traffic lights

Your gut feelings are your internal traffic lights. They tell you whether to go ahead, stop or be cautious. Listen to your gut feeling. If you face a decision – be it about a house, spouse, job or business proposal – and your gut feeling tells you 'no', treat this as a red light, a signal to stop. If you are unsure then honour the feeling; it is probably an amber light telling you to use caution. If so, then you will need to look again at the risks involved and the potential consequences of the decision. You will also need to canvass the views of others. If you understand the pros and cons and you get a green light – your gut feeling tells you to go for it – then do so. This is the source of personal power. You have taken a decision that you believe in and your belief helps to convince others.

If you go ahead when you have received an inner red or amber light then you will probably be troubled by doubts. You may question your motives and the wisdom of your decision and you are more vulnerable to setbacks. All this leads to self-doubt and stress. By contrast, the decisions you feel confident about are likely to fill you with a sense of purpose. Once you commit to a course of action, destiny moves too, as the poet, Goethe, once said. Events conspire to support you in your chosen direction. Setbacks occur, of course, but you have the commitment to overcome them.

Exercise

Make friends with your own internal 'go-ahead', 'caution' and 'stop' signals. Use past experience to explore how they work for you.

◆ Think of a time in your past when you ignored your intuition and took an initiative or followed a course of action that you felt was wrong for you.

◆ Remember the time at which you made the decision, how you felt and what you thought. Take an inventory of your inner experience. Where in your body do you feel the objection signal? Get to know the feeling.

◆ How do you know that your intuition tells you 'no'? Do you get a picture in your mind's eye or does your inner voice sound a warning?

◆ Now think of a time that you took a decision that you were certain was right for you. Choose a decision in which there was some original doubt or pressure was placed on you to change your mind.

◆ Again, relive the moment of decision. Re-experience the gut feeling that told you which course of action to take. Experience that feeling in your body. Get to know it – its location, weight and size.

◆ How do you know that your intuition tells you 'yes'? Do you get a picture in your mind's eye or does your inner voice give you a positive message?

◆ Now take a decision that you face at the moment. What is your gut feeling about it? If you get a red light or somewhere between a red and green light – an amber light – it is warning you to stop and review your decision making. Review the alternatives; look for unconsidered benefits that might offset the disadvantages.

◆ If organizational pressure or your own economic security means that you have to take a course of action that you feel uncomfortable with, then negotiate with yourself. Perhaps you can go with it for a limited period whilst you look for opportunities that feel far more favourable. Negotiate with others involved. Recognize that it could be a source of stress for you and plan ways in which you can relax and dissolve tension.

Building poise

To be convincing to others, the best communicators learn to speak with poise and balance. To their chosen audience they appear calm and in control. When conflict occurs they master it with charm. Their visible state of relaxation is transmitted to others, thereby improving the emotional atmosphere. Investigations into group interactions show that a negative mood can quickly spread, even if it emanates from just one person. But good moods spread just as easily, as people are responsive to subtle emotional cues which indicate the way that others in the group feel about those around them. This is particularly true of group leaders. When you are in the position of addressing or managing a meeting be sure to put yourself into the best possible state of mind.

Regaining control over runaway emotions

We all sometimes feel that our emotions have run away with us. The key thing is to be able to regain control.

Learning to manage anger

> Gerald exploded. He had asked his sales team to suss out the competition, analyze their strengths and weaknesses and recommend ways in which their organization could

emulate the best practices of the opposition. To him, their analysis was banal and their suggestions superficial. He was so incensed he picked up the phone and threw it across the room. Naturally enough, his sales team were cowed and frightened by his response, and cynically humorous about it later. This would not have been so bad if Gerald had not been in the midst of an initiative to improve team-work in the operation he managed. Much good work was undone by this and similar outbursts in the past.

Gerald had the wisdom to recognize he needed help with self-regulation. With the aid of a coach, he identified the triggers for his angry response and how he had been able to control it on the odd occasion in the past. He came to realize that he was often at his worst when he returned from a meeting at the head office, that he was less likely to react angrily if he took a few minutes to relax before a meeting or, indeed, before walking into the premises. He had calmed down in the past by taking ten minutes to walk in the nearby park. When he felt anger besetting him in a meeting he had controlled his feelings by taking a deep breath and sitting on his hands. At the very least, it stopped him picking up the nearest object and hurling it across the room. Using these insights, he began to regulate his emotions and actions better.

Changing from negative states to positive

Gerald took positive action to improve his emotional state in the interests of leadership. Each outburst lost him the trust and respect of the group. To interact effectively with his team he had to learn to substitute poise for anger.

Anxiety, too, interferes with our ability to influence a group. The tell-tale signs of stress or discomfort are picked up intuitively by the audience, which lessens their confidence in the speaker. Lucy, a training consultant, found this to be true when faced with a sceptical and aggressively vocal focus group. Her anxiety betrayed uncertainty and prevented clear thought. As a result, she lost credibility. Had she stayed calm and collected, she would have been able to use her skill and experience to handle the resistance and turn the audience around. Wisely, she consulted a coach who showed her some simple techniques for state control.

Use the same steps as Lucy to maintain a positive state:

◆ Recall a past state of confidence, success or calm.
◆ Relive that good state by stepping into it, seeing, hearing and feeling what was experienced at the time.
◆ When the feeling is at its most intense, link it to an image or colour.
◆ Add on motivational self-talk to the feeling, such as 'I can do it' or 'I am ready for anything'.
◆ Repeat this several times using the same picture and self-talk until you can trigger the state automatically.

Using humour

Humour helps enormously in self-regulation and in raising the mood of the group. Reputedly, an American university has proven that when you smile you feel better – because smiling is linked to the release of endorphins inside the brain. This will be true for both you and your audience. As far as you are able, use humour to release tension in the meeting as soon as you can and smile – sincerely. One of your authors is often asked to speak on psychology to businesspeople and likes to tell the following joke at the start of the talk:

> One manager had an employee who started to go crazy. He wouldn't do any work and sat there at his desk making statues from strange brown substances. The manager walked by and asked what he was making.
>
> 'It's a statue of you!' said the employee.
>
> 'Oh – and what's it made of?'
>
> 'Shit,' said the man.
>
> The manager disciplined him and sent him to the director. The director called a meeting to discuss the problem and when he came into his office there was the employee making another statue.
>
> 'Who's this?' said the director.

'You!' said the man, 'and before you ask – it's made of shit!'

The director decided the man needed help and sent him to the company psychologist. Now this psychologist thought he would play it smarter than the manager and director had and tried an indirect approach. When he saw the man making his statues he said:

'Hi! Is that a statue?'

'Yup.'

'And it's made of shit, right?'

'Yup.'

'And it's a statue of me – right?'

'Nope – not enough shit.'

Jokes like this can defuse the atmosphere at formal gatherings. Of course timing is important – knowing when jokes are useful and when they are best left alone.

As a rule, humour is useful when you need to break down barriers between yourself and others – as in a talk given to an audience.

Building up your poise

If you can stay calm and collected when under pressure, your ability to think clearly will enable you to put your message across in the way you want. Try some of these ways to build up your poise.

◆ Recall times in your past when you have been able to regulate your state well, identify the actions you took that worked and use this insight as a guide to the way to handle pressure in the future.

◆ Prepare to face challenges by recapturing past positive experience and associating the recaptured feelings with a trigger, such as a mental image or positive words you say to yourself. If the challenge comes, thinking of the image or words will trigger the state you want.

◆ Find ways of having fun when you are under stress.

◆ Write down the pros and cons of decisions.

◆ Talk things over with a confidante who may be able to help you get matters in proportion.

◆ Learn to relax. One way is to focus systematically on each muscle group in your body, sense it and then relax the muscles. Start with your feet and move up gradually to the top of your head.

Being persistent and focused

A crucial difference between a top performing salesman in a car dealership and his colleagues was his ability to focus on priorities. In his case, these were attracting sales prospects, selling to as many of them as possible and following up diligently. This was seen to good effect when the salesman continued to phone prospects despite the distractions of his colleagues standing around his desk gossiping, telling jokes, and swapping personal news. He was interested, but not for too long. He possessed an internal 'alarm clock' that kept him on track for bigger priorities. Like many people who have developed persistence, he was self-aware, knew what his goals were, drew confidence from past successes, and regulated himself to achieve more. Above all, he was extremely persistent in developing business leads that would later (despite setbacks) result in success.

Taking the long view

According to Gloria Steinem, rich men plan for the next generation, whilst poor men plan for Saturday night. The longer term your goals, the greater your ability to deal with setbacks and changing circumstances. A long-term view gives you a sense of perspective – useful when problems come along. For example, you may be motivated to provide security for yourself and your family. However, setbacks occur and from time to time you may have to adjust your priorities – such as changing your job, buying a larger home, or moving to a different area. These will take you temporarily from your pursuit of security but, in the long run, the long-term goal will out. And, when success in the short term proves difficult, the vision you have for your family will keep you going. So, enhance your power of persistence by having both short-term and long-term goals, using the latter as the compass when you get lost. This optimistic strategy will help you to weather the odd storm along the way.

Exercise

◆ Think of a time when you were passionately focused on meeting a deadline, achieving a target, or completing a project that was dear to you.
◆ What was important about that task? What key values did you associate with it? Personal development? Learning? Success?
◆ Now focus on the state you were in at that time. What were your thoughts, feelings and actions?
◆ Recall how you shut out any distractions while focusing on the task in hand. What were you *not* aware of any longer?
◆ Chances are that when you recall this state, and the key value attached to it, you will recover the sense of focus that went with it. However – be warned – it won't work unless the project is important to you.

The trick is to balance the longer term perspective with the need to concentrate on day-to-day goals. From time to time you may need to step back from the daily round and connect to your values and priorities. But to maintain credibility with others you also need to be seen to be getting things done. A focused, business-like air builds confidence in others, who are then more likely to respond to your lead.

Looking and sounding credible

From all that we have said so far in this chapter, you will have seen that credibility comes largely from the inside out. Your commitment, focus and resilience will show in your non-verbal communication. Your self-confidence communicates through your body language and voice. There is an alignment between what you think and feel, what you say and how you say it. There is also a skill involved in communicating non-verbally to good effect. It consists in thinking through how you want to put your message across non-verbally. Think about your voice and when it would be useful to:

◆ Speak louder or softer – sometimes a quiet voice is useful because the audience listen harder to it.
◆ Vary the pace at which you speak – slow down to give emphasis to a point you want to make, speed up to portray excitement and conviction.
◆ Vary the tone of your voice – your tone will vary with the speed at which you speak, slowing down will lower the tone of your voice, and a deeper voice can add weight to your words.
◆ Vary the rhythm of speech – a monotonous rhythm can send an audience to sleep just as well as Mogadon.

A relaxed, upright stance or sitting position portrays self-confidence. It is a position from which you can move easily in any direction. Physical balance allows flexibility of thought and movement. Once you move off balance, with weight on one foot or by slouching in a chair, you lose physical and, probably, mental agility. Of course, there are times when it is appropriate to lean back and enjoy a creative conversation – just be sure that your posture suits your communication goal. Think through the way in which you want to use your body language to support your words.

◆ Start meetings on time and adopt a business-like approach.
◆ Relax and sit back when you want an open discussion, sit up when you want to make an important point.
◆ When making a presentation move purposefully, rather than pacing up and down aimlessly. Move towards an audience to grab people's attention and away when you want to turn the heat down. Make contrasting points from different positions: problem in one position, solution in another; 'before' in one position, 'after' in another, for example.
◆ Paint pictures with your hands, rather than simply waving them around. Sometimes people are advised to stop waving their arms about altogether, but this can look wooden.

In summary ...

◆ Create vivid goals for yourself which have emotional value for you. This will give you self-belief which will communicate to others.

◆ Treat your failures and successes as learning opportunities.

◆ Listen to your gut reactions when making important decisions.

◆ Practise developing states of poise, control and humour until they become automatic.

◆ Stay in touch with your most important personal goals and values. This will keep you on track for success.

◆ Improve your credibility by using voice, gesture and movement to emphasize the points you make.

Chapter 3

Reading Others Well

In this Chapter:

- **enhancing your social radar through observation and empathy**
- **how openness to diversity increases your influence**
- **being flexible in the way you perceive others to aid communication**
- **anticipating moods in others so you can read them well.**

African trackers, it is said, rest every now and then, not so much due to the physical effort involved in keeping up with the quarry, but more from mental tiredness. Not only are they following on foot but they are also reading clues, anticipating the target's next move, and mapping out the eventual destination. To do so they have to *become* the game, in a sense, deciding what they would do if they were the animal. This can be taxing in terms of mental and emotional effort.

This analogy tells us something about human communication. To interact effectively we need to develop the art of reading others well. This requires us to put ourselves in the shoes of others, read social cues, and adapt to the culture in which we find ourselves. Expanding our social radar in this way, we become more attuned to the needs and dispositions of others. We can then use this information to gauge our most effective response. It helps if you have a fund of experiences to draw on. Just as travel broadens the mind, so does having experience in relationships, organizations, social and cultural settings, and working practices. If you do not, then you can at least remain open to diversity, using your curiosity as a tool to explore what makes others tick.

Developing empathy

Outstanding communicators sense the mental direction in which people want to move by thinking their thoughts and imagining their feelings. We call this empathy. It is crucial in relationships and face-to-face communication. We might call it informed guesswork, since we can never know for sure what others are really thinking. In this sense reading others well is like doing a jigsaw puzzle: the more links we have the easier it is to fill in the gaps. For example, many people know when their partners are in a low mood. We pick up a series of subtle clues, such as the droop of a shoulder, an absence of eye contact, a change in voice tone, a slower walk. Taking these pieces of the jigsaw together, we compare them with other things we know about this person: that they have a lot on their plate at work, that they have recently got over an illness – and we conclude that they are worried. Although this is informed guesswork, we soon know we are right when we start to ask questions.

Coaches rely on empathy to work out the core issue that most troubles a client. Empathy enables the leader to detect a fall in morale and to take corrective action before it affects performance. It allows top performing car salespeople to see that although they like a car for its style and performance, the customer is more interested in its reliability and safety. Customer representatives rely on their ability to read the thoughts and feelings of customers who are having problems with a service. Of all the skills we have discussed, empathy is perhaps the one most central to emotional intelligence.

Exercise

Who is the best judge of character you know?

Ask the person you have identified how he or she does it. Have them remember a time when they met someone new and were able to reach an accurate judgement quickly.

Questions to ask include:

- What did you do first when you met this person?
- What did you notice first?
- What were you listening for?
- Did this person remind you of other people you have met?
- What was the thing you noticed most about this person?
- What feelings did you develop about the person?
- What did you tell yourself about this person?

Do this for as many 'good judges' as you can and notice the similarities in what they do.

The roots of empathy

The evidence suggests that all human beings are born with a capacity for empathy. This is something we share with other primates like gorillas and chimpanzees: they too spend much time studying their companions and learning to work out what they are thinking and feeling. Children just a few months old seem able to pick up the moods of those around them and mimic them. In fact, this twin ability to observe and imitate behaviour is crucial to child development. Although the ability to empathize can be damaged by poor emotional nurturing in childhood, it can be re-learned. The best conditions in which it can be learned are loving and stable relationships. Against this background, children have the confidence to experiment with new behaviour and learn new social skills. Just as it can be learned, so it can be expanded. The basis for empathy lies in all of us:

◆ our imagination
◆ our ability to read non-verbal signals
◆ our powers of deduction
◆ our ability to infer someone's emotional state from our own experiences when placed in a similar situation.

Exercise

1. Think of a time when you were accurately able to read another person's emotions. For best results pick an occasion when the person was not that well known to you.
2. What did you notice in terms of:
   (a) facial expression
   (b) posture
   (c) gestures
   (d) voice
   (e) the rhythm of speech, or its pauses?
3. Which was the key?
4. Now pick another occasion/person and go through steps 2 and 3 again. Were the clues similar?

Chances are that there were similarities and that you used a combination of clues to make your inference.

Being open to diversity

Being open to diversity allows a breath of fresh air into the fusty corridors of business. We can all become stuck in a rut. Teams develop 'group think' when new team members have to conform to established practices in order to fit in. This has its advantages. The team functions well as a unit and gets its job done efficiently. But it can then become inward-looking and dull. This 'dinosaur effect' happens to companies as well. Those that are lauded start to believe in their own publicity, and last year's innovations become today's rules – set in stone. When this happens companies are vulnerable to competitors who offer new ideas to the same customers. To challenge this tendency, openness is necessary – openness to change, to the market place, to new ways of working, so that existing practices are challenged and improved.

Adapting to cultural diversity

Tolerance is a two-way street. If they are to thrive, organizations need to make room for different cultures. By the same standard, employees need to be open to the organizational culture they operate in. Without giving up your individuality, you will need to match your company culture if you are to succeed. When we fail to match the culture in which other people move it is unlikely (unless the other party is unusually emotionally intelligent) that we will succeed in building a prosperous relationship. Here are some slightly exaggerated examples:

◆ A job-hunter who turns up for an interview at a conservative financial institution dressed in jeans and a t-shirt.

◆ A senior manager who throws her weight around at a team-building exercise.

◆ A customer account manager lunching at the offices of a Far Eastern client who insists on eating 'proper home food'.

◆ An older member of staff who patronises younger team-members and is always comparing present working practices with 'the good old days'.

◆ A salesperson who turns up at a laid-back design agency dressed in a pin-stripe suit.

Openness to diversity goes side by side with empathy in this domain of emotional intelligence. It would be difficult to have one without the other. But where openness leads to curiosity, empathy is the practical skill through which curiosity is channelled. For example, one manager who was assigned to open a new office in Istanbul was selected (although he had little prior experience in this area) for precisely these qualities. The selection panel knew that his openness would make him willing to participate in Turkish culture without preconceptions. His curiosity would lead him to observe, ask questions and understand. This, in turn, would provide him with clues about his new colleagues, which would lead him to empathize with their difficulties.

Overcoming prejudice

The word 'prejudice' simply means 'pre-judgment'. Prejudices block empathy. This closure can be subtle, such as in managers who will only recruit those people who reflect their own behaviours and beliefs. Or it can be gross – as in the examples of people who fail to respect the cultural practices of those around them. Being open to diversity entails a willingness to work with others who are as unlike you as it is possible to be. In their book *First break all the rules*, Marcus Buckingham and Curt Coffman point out that the best managers select people on the basis of talent rather than simply experience and qualification. Given a choice between a talented maverick and a highly qualified and experienced steady performer, they choose the maverick. Why? Their answer is that the maverick is more likely to post outstanding results. Their job is to manage the maverick well. The book's authors call on over a million interviews conducted by the Gallup Organisation and suggest that one of the keys to management success is valuing diversity. The successful managers surveyed differed in age, gender and race. Their management styles differed, too. What they had in common was a readiness to let go of preconceptions and break the rules. They were agents of diversity.

Cultivating an open mind with the people you meet

A common weakness many of us share is to stick to an in-group. We want to stay with people who share our background, our tastes, our opinions, our dress sense, our mannerisms, our politics and our interests. This is understandable but limiting. After a while our social circle only reflects back to us what we think we know. Anything that doesn't fit this narrow social perspective is excluded through prejudice. In time we become narrow-minded and we stagnate. Taken to an extreme, this tendency results in racism, sexism and snobbery.

Yet it is those who are on the fringe – the mavericks and non-conformists – who may have most to teach us. Often they only appear to us to be outsiders because we don't understand the culture they come from, or the one they aspire to. Taking the trouble to talk to them about their aims and assumptions, hopes and wishes, troubles and disappointments soon reveals that they are just people like ourselves. The major difference between them and us lies in the assumptions they make and the perspectives they have developed. Sharing these widens our own horizons and makes it that much more likely we can develop rapport with others who come our way. And we are likely to learn something too.

Understanding a different perspective

Jonathan was a new and inexperienced manager who had been asked to form a project team. Without consultation he was told to include Dan in this team. Dan had a bad reputation as a loner whom others found it difficult to get along with. Although talented, and with success as a trouble-shooter behind him, Dan was far older than Jonathan and had not gone out of his way to be friendly. Jonathan was not looking forward to working with him. One evening, a few days after Dan had joined the team, Jonathan ran into him by chance at a hurling match. While Jonathan was a spectator, Dan was one of the star players! The action was fast and furious and exhilarating to watch. Dan scored twice and Jonathan noticed how he revelled in the action and – most interestingly – played for the team. Afterwards Jonathan went out for a drink with Dan, where he discovered that his first impressions were precisely the opposite of the truth. Dan came from a close-knit community in the West of Ireland where community spirit was a primary virtue. His time in

London had taught him (up to that point) that few English people shared this value so he kept himself to himself. Moreover, he had spent much of his life in the outdoors: sailing, fishing and riding. Fewer still shared these interests or understood his impatience with town life and its neuroses. Learning this, Jonathan treated Dan with new respect and went out of his way to include Dan in the team. Having listened to what Dan had to say about team spirit, Jonathan also took care to organize team events – on one occasion asking Dan to arrange a day out sailing a yacht in the Channel. Knowing more about the perspective through which Dan viewed things, he learned more tolerance for Dan's behaviour.

Most of us, at one time or another, are tempted to reject non-conformists like Dan. Be aware of this tendency and question your judgement when you come up against people who stand apart from the rest. Is it because the person is genuinely disruptive or is it because they are simply different? Old work practices and modes of thinking become habits. These habits need to be questioned from time to time to make sure they do not become fossilised.

In business every organization needs a mix of people to be successful. Each team needs an organizer who gets things done, an analyst who thinks through the difficulties ahead, a harmonizer who co-ordinates effort, and people with warmth and humour who bind the team together. But what is also important is the creative person who comes up with new perspectives and new ideas that enable the team to grow. Interestingly, it is often this kind of person most teams lack. Perhaps every organization should be compelled by law to employ a certain number of 'misfits'. Channelled in the right way, their contributions would keep it emotionally healthy.

Working with new perspectives

The Native American Hopi people say that to know a warrior you must learn to walk a mile in his moccasins. This means walking, thinking and sensing in the same way as the other person does. Effective communicators rely on their ability to read the intentions of people they encounter. It is not simply an intellectual game of weighing up someone's strengths and weaknesses. It means adopting their viewpoint so that you can help in the search for common ground.

So, one useful perspective in communication is from the standpoint of the listener. When you prepare for a meeting, imagine you are the person you are meeting to find out how they might think and feel about an issue. If you meet their needs as well as your own, your ideas and suggestions are more likely to be accepted. Occasionally during the meetings take a moment to imagine how your colleague is thinking and feeling. You will get a sense of how you can adapt to improve the communication.

Another useful perspective is to look at and listen to an interaction from a detached viewpoint, as if you were your own coach. To do this try the exercise below.

Exercise

♦ Imagine that you are watching a scene being played out on a theatre stage. On stage at the moment is a person who causes you problems of some kind. As you look at the person on stage, he or she enacts the behaviour that you find difficult.

♦ Give the behaviour a name. Your label might be: 'insensitive', 'gossip', 'self-centred', 'aggressive', 'lazy' or 'complaisant'. Choose a label that sums up the behaviour you see and hear on stage.

♦ Now, you see another person walk on stage. Your 'difficult' person interacts in the same problematic way with this new person. As you look closer at the two people, you see that the second person is you.

♦ Label your behaviour and notice the ways in which your actions and words in some ways stimulate or encourage the 'difficult' person's behaviour. Your label for your own behaviour might be: 'doormat', 'defensive', 'compliant', 'easily pleased', 'timid' or 'detached'.

♦ Now ask yourself how you could change your behaviour so that you would have a productive relationship with this other person. Give your new set of behaviours a label like 'tolerant', 'flexible', 'humorous', 'assertive', 'creative' or 'wild'.

♦ Re-run the whole scenario on the stage noticing how your new behaviours affect the other person in a more positive way.

♦ Carry out the last two steps several times, using different sets of behaviours, until you have a good mix of possible responses to choose from.

This sort of mental theatre can revolutionize our understanding of a situation because we see how we contribute to a problem. This enables us to take action to improve the situation, rather than blaming others for it.

Detecting moods

From the very earliest weeks of a child's life it moves in harmony with its mother's voice. It seems that this non-verbal communication is one way in which a baby cements its relationship with its mother. Studies have shown that spouses have a better insight into their husband or wife's emotional state if they reflect their partner's posture and movement. Counsellors acquire an understanding of their clients' states of mind if they mirror their body language and voice. Salespeople get a better sense of their potential clients if they match their mood non-verbally – if their client is brisk, they are brisk, if their client is relaxed, they are relaxed. Matching gives a profound insight to the emotional state of the person matched. And, by the way, it happens quite naturally. People tend to match non-verbally when they are getting on well together. It is a useful yardstick for rapport.

Exercise

Look at these figures. Which of them would you say had rapport?

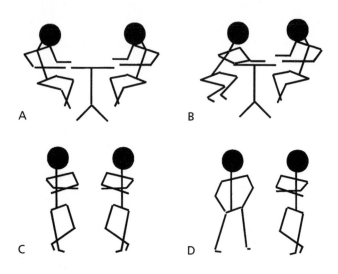

A   B

C   D

Answer

Only figures A and C are matching – a sign that they have rapport.

So far, we have covered two ways of detecting people's moods in communication.

- ◆ The first is to step into their shoes to take the imaginative leap needed to empathize with their thoughts and feelings.
- ◆ The second is to match their non-verbal communication – voice and body language – to sense how they are feeling.

Anticipating reactions

In a training programme that we run, we ask participants to carry out an exercise in which they communicate three different emotions. However, the difficult part is that they have to use the same banal words each time. If you think that is easy, try saying 'Shopping day is Saturday' while conveying:

(a) exhilaration

(b) anger

(c) surprise.

It seems simple but, first time out, trainees often find it difficult to get both the message and the mood over to the others. Success comes when they learn to dramatize their non-verbal behaviours. The problem also occurs when the audience fails to read the non-verbal communication accurately. The exercise is thus a two-way training: the actors expand their repertoire of non-verbal cues while the audience becomes more sensitive to them.

Some research suggests that, in certain contexts, over 90% of the meaning of a message lies in the non-verbal communication – voice tone and body language – rather than in the words. We respond non-verbally without thinking about it. Other studies have shown that our facial response to an emotional stimulus happens within milli-seconds. Sigmund Freud said that we can keep no secrets; even if our voice is silent, we chatter with our fingertips.

Since accurate communication relies on the ability to interpret non-verbal messages you will do well to observe the responses you get. Here are some of the most important:

Posture
Laid back or forward
Relaxed or tense
Rigid or flexible
Still or restless
Erect or hunched
Legs crossed or uncrossed
Head up or down
Shoulders tense or relaxed

Movement
Jerky or smooth
Definite or hesitant
Foot/finger tapping or still

Breathing
Deep or shallow
Smooth or jerky

Facial expression
Tense or relaxed
Pale or flushed
Eyebrows up or down
Mouth smiling or straight
Brow furrowed or smooth

Eyes
Still or moving
Looking up or down

Eye contact or looking away
Focused or defocused
Bright or dull

Voice
Loud or quiet
Quick or slow
High or low pitched
Rhythmic or arrhythmic
Varied or monotonous

All these are clues that rely just as much on what changes as on what is observed. Learn to look for those changes. If a person has been leaning back and then leans forward, it may betray a change in thinking. It is a sign that you may need to ask a question to find out what is happening. It is risky to leap to conclusions based on non-verbal communication alone. Make your conclusions tentative so that you keep an open mind. Ask a question to find out the reason behind a particular non-verbal response.

Exercise

You are talking to a colleague, who suddenly leans back and frowns. Which of the questions below would be most useful to find out the reason for the response?

(a) What's the problem?
(b) Do you disagree?
(c) How do you feel about what we have been saying?

Answer

Question (a) makes the dangerous assumption that there is a problem. It may seem an intrusive assumption about your colleague's reaction and could provoke a defensive response.

Question (b) is also an attempt at mind reading, implying that your colleague disagrees with you. It is also a closed question, so may elicit little information other than 'yes' or 'no'.

Question (c) is an open question that does not assume that you have read your colleague's mind. It is the most useful of the three and is most likely to yield a helpful answer.

When you have expanded your openness to the cultural assumptions, moods and perspectives of others and refined your capacity for empathy, you are in a position to rehearse your interactive skills when holding specific meetings. Anticipating the reactions of others, you can mentally rehearse your meetings until you are sure that your actions and words are as convincing as possible.

A dress rehearsal

> Geri had experienced very little success in convincing her line manager, the head of training, to take up her ideas. This time, she felt, things would be different. She would look at her idea from her manager's viewpoint. It would at least give her a sporting chance of predicting and pre-empting her manager's objections to her latest proposal – to introduce online training in management

skills to the company.   She brought her
manager to mind and then rehearsed the
arguments she would put in favour of the new
initiative. Next she imagined the response of
her manager. To do this she made the
imaginative leap of becoming the manager.
She adopted the sort of posture her manager
typically adopted when he listened to new
ideas. She tried, as far as she could, to respond
to her own proposals as her manager would.
As her manager, she was concerned that
people would not be motivated to finish a
course that they started. She felt that people
might acquire knowledge but not the
understanding needed to put people skills into
practice. She worried about the problems of
selling the idea to line managers for whom
this would be a trip into the unknown and to
a sceptical personnel director who gained
kudos from the success of the company's
conventional training. Still looking at it from
her manager's position, she was concerned
about the department losing control of the
training process. And, finally, she was aware
of the manager's fear of being found wanting
with a technology he knew little about. On
the upside, she sensed an interest in a new
idea and the possible payoff that could follow
a successful introduction of a new approach to
training. Saving on conference centre costs
was also attractive. These insights persuaded
her to change her normal way of presenting

> new ideas. Instead of extolling the virtues of
> the new approach, she decided to start with its
> pros and cons and address each of the
> predicted concerns.

Geri was, of course, engaged in an act of imagination and some of her predictions may have been adrift. But her preparation was an act of empathy.   It gave her a far better idea of her manager's thinking and a far better chance of persuading him to buy into her ideas.

To anticipate objections:

◆ Bring the person to be influenced to mind (or an influential and sceptical member of a group that you need to convince).
◆ Imagine the conversation you will have with the person concerned.
◆ Then, step into the person's shoes – think as if you were him or her.
◆ As that person, imagine your response – how you will feel and what you will think, what you will accept and what you will reject.
◆ Build this insight into your plan for the communication.

In summary ...

◆ Use empathy to work out the other person's needs, intentions and goals.

◆ Be open to diversity and be ready to work with people who break the rules.

◆ Seek to understand, and then to adapt to the culture of, the organizations and people you work with.

◆ Use the perspectives of others, or of neutral observers, to reflect on and improve the way you act in meetings.

◆ Match the moods of others by subtly reflecting back their movements, gestures and voice quality.

◆ Anticipate negative reactions from others by rehearsing their likely responses to your proposals. Then come up with some answers for them.

Chapter 4

Persuasive Communication

In this Chapter:

◆ **how your emotions work as signals to take action**

◆ **the link between your emotions and your most important values in life**

◆ **how you can communicate attractively by utilizing others' values**

◆ **creating proposals that others want to listen to**

◆ **dealing with objections through the careful use of active listening.**

In this chapter we look at how you can communicate in a way that is immediately appealing to your audience. People are persuaded by emotions as well as by arguments that make sense to them. Understanding the link between emotional appeal and the values that people use to distinguish what is important to them will give you the basis for persuasive communication. When you learn to read your own emotional reactions, and those of others, you are in a position to refine your presentations so that they have maximum impact.

Emotions as codes

Emotions are complex and fascinating. They convey more
information than words can ever do. They are, in fact, codes.
They provide clues to past experiences, memories,
associations and assumptions. Subtle expressions and gestures,
pauses and hesitations in conversation, a glance of the eye –
all have an indefinable way of holding the attention.
Thousands of bits of information are passed through the
nervous system by eye and ear. They are evaluated by both
the thinking and emotional centres, which then pass on
hormonal information to the gut, the muscles and nerves.
All this happens in a few milliseconds and provides us with
an emotional signal that we now have to interpret.

Paying attention to feelings

Steven was a manager in a financial
institution in the City of London. He ran a
team of traders in the busy options sector.
Due to a reorganization he was asked to work
alongside another manager co-operating on
the same customer base. His first impression
of his new colleague was uncomfortable.
Although Jack was perfectly charming Steven
felt that something wasn't 'right' about Jack.
But he suppressed his feelings in the interests
of harmony and good working relationships.
In the months that followed, Jack went out of
his way to be friendly and even invited Steven
and his girlfriend to his wedding. Whenever
he saw Steven he never failed to ask him how

he was and whether he could help in any way. However, Steven was soon made redundant while Jack took over his job. Confidentially, he was told by one of the directors that Jack had been undermining him behind his back 'from day one' – never losing an opportunity to draw the attention of the directors to Steven's mistakes.

A couple of years later Steven, now working for another company, was asked to report to a newly-appointed manager following a promotion. As soon as they met Steven experienced an uncanny feeling of edginess in his back and throat. It was the same feeling he had had on meeting Jack. Paying attention to his feelings this time, Steven began to look for another job. Not before time. A few weeks after leaving he learned that this particular manager had a bad reputation for taking the credit for his juniors' successes while unloading onto them the blame for his own failures.

One way to think about an emotional response is that it is an unconscious summary of all the things we have ever learned about a particular subject. An emotion brings together memories, beliefs, feelings, thoughts and learned ideas in a single response. Steven's uncanny feeling of edginess could not have been put into words, but it was a danger flag he did well to pay attention to.

You may recall that the word 'emotion' comes from an original Latin root word for 'movement'. Emotions do indeed move us either away from or towards people or situations. Our feeling of disgust moves us away from putrid food because we have learned to associate it with illness. Our feeling of joy, on the other hand, moves us towards babies because we associate them with innocence and new life. Similarly, sadness moves us away from thoughts of loss, and anger moves us towards something that we perceive as a threat – so that we try to reduce it in size. These internal movements are signals for us to consider and take action. They also contain wisdom. When we consider emotions as codes, we gain insight into Pascal's saying that 'the heart has reasons which Reason knows nothing of'. Each emotion is a logical organization of thoughts, neurological reactions and stored pieces of learning into a single response. And it is expressed with beautiful economy.

Emotions and values

Emotions are closely linked to values. We have seen how emotions move us towards and away from situations. The reason for this is that we evaluate things in positive or negative ways. Consider this list of positive and negative evaluations:

Positive	**Negative**
Happy	Miserable
Supportive	Snide
Attractive	Unattractive
Wise	Foolish
Kind	Hateful
Helpful	Obstructive

What will be your emotions on encountering someone whom you evaluate as being from the first list, and someone whom you evaluate from the second list?

Let us recall the case of Elliott mentioned in Chapter 1. His surgery – to remove a brain tumour – severed the connections between the decision-making centres in the brain and his emotional brain. As a result, every time he was called upon to make a decision he was left with no feelings about them either way. His capacity to assign a *value* to each decision and generate a 'gut feel' for them was gone. One thing was just as important as another and so was everything else. Lacking the capacity for values he could not motivate himself to do anything in particular, or to stick with it when he hit setbacks. What was worse, the negative consequences of his actions made no difference either. No matter how many warnings he received, or how many times he was fired from a job, there was no special reason for him to do better next time.

Elliott is an extreme case. However, it is true to say that some of us are better at reading our emotions and values than others. This intrapersonal skill is often linked to the corresponding interpersonal skill – the ability to recognize, and engage with, other people's values. Nevertheless, it is a skill that can be developed.

Exercise

1. Suppose you only had a year left to live. What activities would you focus on during that time? Write down those activities.
2. Now ask yourself which activities you would focus on if you only had three months left. Write down these activities.
3. Do the same for the list of things you would do if you only had a week left to live.
4. Now rank the activities you have written down in order of importance. You may find that the activities on the 'one week' list give you clues concerning the priorities in your life.
5. Take the first item on the list and ask yourself – what is important about this? Write down the answer. Now ask yourself – why is *that* important? Keep on using this question for each answer until you cannot think of a higher value. (You may find that your answers eventually begin to sound the same – e.g. you put down 'Helping Children' and that was important because you had the value 'Family' and that was important because you had the value 'Love' but your next answer was 'Devotion' which is really based on 'Love' – so Love becomes your highest value for that activity.
6. Repeat step 5 for every item on your list until you have a complete description of all your most

important values. You can use the list of values below to help you with this.

Key values

Success	Integrity	Love	Service
Security	Self-improvement	Creativity	Wealth
Community	Wonder	Prestige	Compassion
Originality	Knowledge	Pleasure	Recognition
Peace	Justice	Professionalism	Happiness
Satisfaction	Family	Empowerment	Truth
Choice	Quality	Spirituality	Health
Sharing	Innovation	Beauty	Helping
Wisdom	Desirability	Fame	Forgiveness

Personal integrity – through which others learn to trust what you say and thereby become more willing to follow your lead – lies in knowing what your most important values are. By planning your life so that you find ways to fulfil them, and avoiding situations that violate them, you will be half-way to becoming a persuasive communicator. The other half of the journey lies in linking your proposals to the values of others.

Utilizing values

Other things being equal, and given a free choice, most people will be persuaded to do something if it has value to them to do so. A person's values give an emotional tone to the choice that may well make it irresistible. Note that persuasion depends on the speaker's ability to empathize with the other person, discern their important values, and adapt the message to their preferences. Persuasion is not a one-way street: it depends on give and take.

The process of give and take is evident in commerce. Many stores and mail-order companies now offer free gifts and discounts in return for purchases. Some charities also provide free gifts in return for your support, with the added bonus that contributors will also satisfy the important social value of helping others less fortunate themselves. Emotionally intelligent salespeople are also aware of how reciprocity creates a platform for sales. When buying a new car it is common for people to be offered a choice between an expensive model and a cheaper one. Saying no to the expensive car often leads to a request to consider the alternative. If this is presented, also, as a way of satisfying the buyer's values (for example, it is cost-effective, reliable, and designed for the family) then the choice becomes extremely attractive. The give and take of saying no to one thing and yes to another leaves the buyer feeling in control of the transaction.

Arbitrating the best available deal

Brian and Duncan were in conflict over the merger of their respective teams in a corporate reorganization. They had been asked to decide between them on job redundancies, the allocation of new responsibilities and who (if either of them) would lead the new team. It was made clear to both that, should they fail to reach agreement, an appointment would be made over their heads. They could agree on none of these and, finding that they could make little headway in their negotiations, they called in Sally, a mediator with experience in conflict resolution. Her first move was to interview both managers individually and ask each to write down their priorities for the merger. Duncan produced a list that read:

1. Fairness in deciding redundancies and role allocations
2. Restoration of staff morale
3. Authority

Brian's list had just two items:

1. Seniority
2. A productive team

Sally noticed that both lists contained related values, as fairness and the restoration of morale led to a productive team. Pointing this out to both led them to agree that Duncan would decide on redundancies using length of service, specialist knowledge, and recent performance grades as criteria. The second issue was more difficult as both wanted to be the senior manager. However, Duncan stressed that he valued authority because most of the people in the new team would be members of his old team and would be used to his ways. Brian, on the other hand, valued seniority because it would mean career advancement. On this basis (anything else would lead to neither getting what they wanted), Sally

> eventually negotiated for Brian to have
> seniority while Duncan had responsibility for
> the day-to-day running of the team.

Emotionally intelligent communicators pay attention to others' values because they know that people are motivated (that is, moved, or emoted) by the things that matter to them. They therefore take care to find a way to link people's values to the outcomes they propose. Duncan and Brian, placed in a difficult situation, were able to change a no-win situation into a partial win for both by having their attention drawn to the things that most mattered to them.

Establishing key values

There is an old maxim: 'Do unto others as you would be done by'. But it is perhaps more realistic to say (as Bernard Shaw did) 'Do not treat others as you would yourself. Their tastes may not be the same.' Different people have different values. Fairness is important to some people in a negotiation, whilst winning is important to others. Some want the lowest possible price when buying; others want the highest available quality. Some want freedom of choice and variety in a job; for others status and high earnings are more important. Some people like clarity when they receive a task or assignment; others prefer a broad goal that leaves them to fill in the detail. Rapport and influence are easier if you can find out people's values and reflect them in your communication. You can find out people's values by asking questions and listening to the answers.

Exercise

Try this with a friend. Identify some activity such as a hobby, interest, or sport your friend follows regularly. Then ask:

- What is most important to you about doing that?
- What do you mean by (value)? (To clarify answer, if needed.)
- And what do you get from having *that* (value)?
- And why is having *that* (second value) important?

You can ask these questions several times (but not too often) until you get the core value to which your friend attaches the most importance. Doing this for a number of activities will reveal some of the most important values in your friend's life.

Understanding other people's values

> Richard felt that he had not been sufficiently assertive in his meeting with an influential line manager. As a training manager, he depended for success on the active involvement of the managers in his initiatives. Yet he was often frustrated by his inability to secure their support. He felt he articulated his case clearly and put it over confidently, so what was the problem?
>
> He decided to take his own medicine and attend a course that stressed the importance

of values in influencing people and taught the three questions set out above. He realized where he had been going wrong. He had developed what he thought was a compelling case, but it failed to reflect the needs and criteria of the line managers. He realized that he needed to find out more about what they actually wanted and then to adapt his message to suit the person. On his return to work, he used the questioning techniques given above to:

◆ find out the value underlying a line manager's thinking on a particular subject.
◆ find out what the manager meant by the key words given to avoid rash assumptions about the meaning of a particular word.
◆ find out the higher values which lay behind managers' decisions.
◆ accommodate these values in his explanations and proposals.

Rehearsing outcomes

Think back for a moment to the example of Peter and James in Chapter 1. James respects the perspectives, intentions and values of others and is flexible enough to build a case which takes into account those factors. Peter, by contrast, has no respect for the position of his opponents. He does not have the emotional maturity to distinguish between intentions and behaviour. Instead he assumes that all opposition is directed at him personally. This prevents him coming up with arguments that might get at least some of his proposals accepted – or withdrawing from a lost cause and finding a more productive one. The ability to stand back from our cherished ideas and consider them objectively, as others will do, is a key to persuasive argument.

Rehearsing for a difficult situation

Jane was not looking forward to the Board meeting. She had recently been appointed a director and was the only woman on the board. She was aware that her appointment had caused some resentment and had already been forced to deal with some snide remarks from some of her fellow directors. Now the chief executive had asked her to make her first presentation on a controversial cost-cutting proposal at the next meeting. She knew that the proposal would mean reduced budgets for each of the departments represented at the meeting. And what was worse – she hated having to make presentations. Although she accepted that they went with the job she would have preferred to present her ideas in a more informal setting.

Luckily she had one ally on the Board – an older colleague with many years' experience of corporate in-fighting. He told her that rehearsal was nine-tenths of the battle. 'If you can cover every angle, every likely objection – and have an answer for all of them – you will come up trumps.' Together they mentally rehearsed what every single person there would be likely to say. Jane discovered on the way that some of the objections she imagined were good ones and so she changed her proposals in order to account for them. She realised, too, that, despite their poor behaviour towards her, many of her colleagues were motivated by important values connected to the well being of the organization. So she slipped in some key points to show how her ideas would preserve such important values as efficiency, customer service, teamwork, and the survival of the company. After a week going over the meeting many times, she was as well prepared as it was possible to be. To her surprise, many of the most important objections she rehearsed were never mentioned. She learnt later (from the chief executive, who was highly complimentary) that her performance had been so commanding that opposition fell flat.

As Jane's colleague knew, rehearsal is the basis for all really effective communication. Notice how Jane used empathy to anticipate the potentially hostile responses of her colleagues. Notice, too, how she was careful to adapt her proposals to match their most important values. Rehearsing your outcomes through empathy is a direct application of emotional intelligence to the work place.

Exercise

1. Think of a meeting (either one-on-one or in a group) that either is coming up or could come up in the near future. The trickier the meeting the better.
2. Now think about ONE thing you would like to achieve at that meeting. Be sure to make your goal realistic – i.e. something that is possible for you to achieve under your own steam. Do NOT pick a goal which is outside your control like 'getting people to agree with me'. Instead, choose a target like stating a point, putting up a good argument, looking confident, staying relaxed, or setting the agenda.
3. Now imagine that you are physically there at the meeting, achieving your goal. What are you doing, thinking, feeling, saying? Allow your imagination free rein just as if anything were possible for you.
4. Now – one by one – imagine you are looking through the eyes of each of the others at the meeting, observing your actions. What are 'you' thinking and feeling about this performance? What else would you like to see or hear. How might your performance be improved? If necessary, guess your colleagues' answers.
5. Now re-run step 3, this time improving it to meet any objections you encountered or improvements desired.
6. You can rehearse this as many times as you need to. You can also imagine having a trusted mentor with you in your imaginary rehearsal giving you supportive advice.

Developing your point

Ancient orators in classical times were guided by three rules of communication in addressing an audience: build a strong argument, develop credibility, and find a way to create an emotional appeal for what is said. These are still good rules to apply now. In this section we will look at building an argument that engages your audience emotionally as well as intellectually.

In developing your point there are four rules to observe:

◆ Be factual and objective.
◆ Be open and honest.
◆ State positive consequences.
◆ Ask for a commitment.

Being factual and objective

The key here is to give evidence for the thinking behind your proposals. Avoid vagueness and generalizations. Instead of saying 'Recent performance has been poor', say 'Our sales figures last month were 30% short of our agreed targets'. Wherever possible, mention specific events or facts known to your listeners.

Being open and honest

Most people have enough emotional intelligence to notice when someone is evasive or uncomfortable. If you have doubts about your argument then tackle the issue head-on by mentioning them and (if appropriate) asking for ideas from others. This will mean your developing a dialogue with your audience. For example, if you are the sales team manager commenting on low sales, but you also know that the team is working as hard as it can, then you should include this in your address: 'I know we are all working really hard as it is so we will have to think about how we can work smarter as well as harder'.

State positive consequences

When you have thought through your argument, consider what will be the benefits to your listeners. Tapping into their values will also help. Then be explicit in stating what those are. For example: 'If we can improve our sales figures then that will make us the sales leaders in this organization and that means we'll be in line for those bonuses.'

Ask for a commitment

At the end of each proposal, ask for your audience to do something, no matter how small. A commitment could be to agree with what was said, volunteer for action, provide feedback, offer support, or to come back with more information.

The complete example is:

> 'Our sales figures last month were 30% short of our agreed targets. I know we are all working really hard as it is, so we will have to think about how we can work smarter as well as harder. If we can improve our sales figures then that will make us the sales leaders in this organisation and that means we'll be in line for those bonuses. Now – when can we all meet to discuss this?'

Active listening

In order to deal with interruptions, tangential responses, misunderstandings and unforeseen objections, effective communicators are ready to develop a dialogue with their listeners. The skill of active listening is important here. People with this skill bracket off their own preconceptions and allow themselves to be absorbed in what is said, using questions every step of the way to build a complete picture of the other person's position. A useful mnemonic for active listening is EARS – Empathize, Acknowledge, Reflect, Summarize.

Empathize – mentally stepping into the other person's shoes to gather information about their emotions, thoughts and assumptions.

Acknowledge – letting the other person know that their concerns and needs are heard and understood.

Reflect – mirroring back key phrases (particularly those linked to values) in what is said. Also matching some aspects of body language.

Summarize – summarizing frequently to check understanding and then asking a question or making a proposal that leads to positive action.

If you are interrupted or you meet with an objection when making a presentation or holding a meeting, stop for a moment and use active listening. Seek to distinguish between the way in which the other party is making their point, and the intention behind it. For example, a senior manager might seem brusque or even rude. This may come across to you as a sweeping dismissal of your ideas. However, emotionally intelligent interaction means keeping your cool while searching for the values, needs and purposes that lie behind communication.

Listening for key words and phrases

Very often, the clues are in the words themselves. Listen out for 'hot' words that reveal the speaker's concerns and interests. Often these will the same, or similar to, the value terms shown in the box earlier in this chapter. Be sure to use exactly the same words in the reply you make.

Active listening

Here is a sample dialogue showing active listening in action. Marion is a surveyor making a presentation to a group of team leaders on a long-term project which is designed to improve the quality of the company's supply chain to its customers. Notice the way in which Marion uncovers the emotive interests that lie behind Geoff's interruption.

Marion *(concluding)*: One of the important things we will need to do to make this project work is to appoint a liaison officer from each team so that we can co-ordinate our efforts ...

Geoff: Wait a minute. This sounds like another demand that's been placed on the teams. You've already said we're going to have to provide you with reports, find new sites, install a telephone connection, go to monthly meetings, and now we're going to have to take someone off other projects so they can liaise with your team.

Marion *(empathizing)*: I can understand how it might seem as if we are placing extra demands on your team in the short term. In the long term it will ease the pressures you're having to face right now.

Geoff: Yeah, yeah I got that. But it's those short-term pressures that are the problem right now. My team are already stretched to the limit. How can we maintain quality of service if we give them more work to do today?

Marion *(reflecting and speaking faster in order to match the urgency in Geoff's voice)*: It sounds like you're worried about the overload of work in your team and maintaining quality of service. How can we deal with those issues and make this project a success? After all, this is the reason we are doing this – to reduce the work-load on people over the long term and improve quality.

Geoff *(beginning to calm down)*: Yeah – and I support that. But I am still responsible for the morale of my team. They're not going to like what I've heard today.

Marion *(summarizing then making a proposal)*: Your team's morale comes first and we have to find a way to support them in the work they're doing now and make this project work. How about if I came round to meet your team, explained this project to them, and asked for their ideas? Would that suit you?

Geoff: That would be a life-saver.

In order to get a fair hearing for her proposals, Marion needed to respond to the emotional concern Geoff felt for his team. She did this by reflecting back Geoff's worries and asking open-ended questions about how these could be addressed while also ensuring the success of the project. In offering to meet Geoff's team she makes a proposal that is a first step towards achieving both goals. Marion's influence has worked through give and take; a mixture of assertiveness and empathy.

In summary ...

♦ **Be alert to your 'uncomfortable' feelings – they may be your best advisors.**

♦ **Your 'gut reactions' are powerful aids to decision-making – use them well.**

♦ **To motivate yourself for long-term success, stay close to the projects and values that mean the most to you.**

♦ **Motivate others by identifying values that motivate them.**

♦ **Rehearse meetings by finding a way to link your ideas to your audience's values.**

♦ **Structure your proposals by sticking to the facts, being open about difficulties, stating the positive consequences and asking for commitment.**

◆ **Deal with objections through active listening –
empathy, acknowledging concerns, reflecting
back key phrases and summarizing.**

Chapter 5

Managing Conflict

In this Chapter:

◆ **substituting cool reason for emotion when tempers run high**

◆ **controlling fear and anger**

◆ **understanding the basis of fear and anger**

◆ **finding other ways to view old problems**

◆ **finding common ground with others through dialogue.**

In this book we have argued that coming to terms with your own and others' emotions is the key to good communication. This does not mean that all emotions are good. Nor are we arguing that the expression of emotion is a substitute for logical thinking, taking action and getting results. There are times when you may need to sideline your emotions (at least temporarily) in order to get things done. At other times you may need to ignore the emotions of others in order to make your point. There is an art, too, to controlling emotions.

Jackie keeps her cool

Jackie was a junior manager at a retail
company supplying computers and other hi-tec
equipment. A big order from one of the
organization's largest and most prestigious
buyers had gone horribly wrong, with a
potential loss of millions of pounds. Sub-
standard equipment had been supplied and
the buyer was now threatening to cancel all its
contracts. As one of the managers originally
involved in shipping the order, she had been
told to attend a top-level meeting of senior
managers to be chaired by the managing
director. The purpose of the meeting was to
establish what was to be done to resolve the
issue and retain the contract.

From the first, the managing director tore into
the assembled staff around the room. One by
one, each of the managers was grilled about
their part in the fiasco with heated and
peremptory questions. The chief would brook
no explanations and steadily grew more and
more sarcastic. It really seemed that his main
purpose was to humiliate everyone there as
much as he could. Two senior managers who
were brave enough to answer back were
treated to withering contempt. Soon the chief
was shouting at the top of his voice to a
cowed and silent audience.

Jackie put up her hand. All eyes were on her. The chief paused and waited for her to begin. Speaking up she reminded him of the purpose of the meeting and asked if they could go on to consider practical remedies for the problem. Glaring at Jackie, the chief began angrily to cross-examine her about her part in the affair. She dealt with all his questions in the same level voice, never wavering in her eye-contact. She admitted mistakes had been made but that the company now needed to consider how to retain the client's business. She had a proposal to make and wanted to find out his views on it. She coolly repeated this point until, gradually, he began to calm down and the meeting turned to practical matters.

A few months later, Jackie was promoted at the recommendation of the managing director. He commented that she had caught his eye at that meeting with her 'positive' and 'business-like' attitude.

Jackie refused to be swept along with the tide of fear and anger that was engulfing the meeting. She stood out because of her coolness and eye to business. After a time, her calmness communicated itself first to the managing director and then to the rest of the group. To diffuse escalating conflict she tapped into the underlying purpose of the meeting and recalled it to its goal. Her emotional intelligence consisted in *not* giving way to negative emotion and keeping the goal in mind.

The basis of fear and anger

These two very different emotions are not that dissimilar in origin. Both are linked to the 'fight or flight' response mechanisms which promote survival. But where anger is linked to 'fight', fear is connected with 'flight' (sometimes, also, to the 'freeze' response which keeps you where you are while your mind works out what to do next). When it detects a threat the emotional alarm system floods the nervous system with hormones which send a rush of energy through the body. This arousal surge peaks in just a few minutes and puts the body into a hair-trigger state of readiness. Meanwhile, working just a little slower, the thinking centres consider the stimulus and, if it is found disturbing, activate the thalamus. This then sends signals to raise the level of stress hormones in the bloodstream. These hormones also raise blood pressure and heart rate, constrict the chest, open the sweat glands, and create changes in the gut and a dry mouth.

So far, the reactions for anger and fear are closely similar. Much of the difference in quality between the two is caused by the appraisals that go with each experience. Typically, anger is externally focused on obstacles for which others carry the responsibility and comes with thoughts of resentment, recrimination and blame. Fear, meanwhile, is related to the self and is associated with uncertainty, worry and dread.

The problem is that your emotional brain does not pay attention to the actions you take; instead it continues to press the alarm repeatedly. This gets in the way of reflection and planning. It is vital, therefore, that you find some ways of disengaging from emotion while you do these things. When involved in conflict this skill is imperative. The key is to take some time out to analyze what your emotions are telling you and then, from a detached viewpoint, plan your next move.

In situations where others are being overwhelmed by emotions, it is vital that you do not take that as a comment on your behaviour. Jackie was able to separate her managing director's anger from the question of her competence in the job. Doing this enabled her to press her point about the need for positive action rather than recriminations. She exercised good judgement in a way that made an emotional response from her unnecessary.

Disengaging from fear

Emotional intelligence is not just about *expressing* emotions. It is also a matter of *controlling* them. As we saw earlier, emotions result from super-fast interchanges between the thinking centres and the more primitive instinctive centres in the brain. Positive emotions are linked to our most deeply held values and priorities. However, negative emotions are usually linked to fear and anger. While we need to cherish positive emotions, negative emotions are rarely helpful. Sometimes fear prevents us from doing something that is genuinely dangerous, like picking up a poisonous snake, and anger can be channelled into positive action, such as fighting injustice. But more often, fear and anger are destructive forces in our lives.

Fear merely blocks us from taking action. If the fear is realistic then all we need to do is change our plans and the fear disappears. Often our fears are based on nothing more than imagination. We build up catastrophes in our head which are based on the worst possible thing that could happen – and then add on a few more disasters for good measure. Over 50 years ago an American study surveyed people's fears and then asked them a few weeks later what had happened to them. It was found that over 90% of the events feared had not actually happened at all, while about 7% had happened to some extent – but nothing like the disasters imagined.

Of course there are things in life that we are afraid of but can't avoid – ageing, financial loss, accidents, war, illness and separations. But, considered realistically, these are the price we pay for being alive. Approaching them with fear will make them worse than they need to be. Approaching them with acceptance and a trust in our ability to cope with things empowers us to meet these challenges head-on.

It seems that in human beings, fear is contagious because it is fuelled by imagination. To overcome our inborn tendency to be dominated by fear, we need to use our imagination constructively. Instead of frightening ourselves with the worst that can happen, it is better to imagine how we are going to deal with it.

Exercise

◆ Take something you fear will happen in the future.
◆ Now *realistically* work out the best scenario, the worst, and the most likely outcome.
◆ Take the worst-case scenario and imagine yourself dealing with it at your very best. Imagine how you will cope even if this happens.
◆ Now take the most likely outcome. Imagine yourself dealing with *that* to the best of your abilities.
◆ Take the most likely outcome once more and ask yourself: What can I do *now* to make it less likely that some of these things will happen, or to prepare myself for this?

As Susan Jeffers, in her book *Feel the Fear and Do it Anyway,* reminds us, fear will be with us no matter what we do – so we might as well get on with making the best decisions we can.

Snuffing out frustration

In a particularly fine passage in his book *Emotional Intelligence,* Goleman describes how anger is linked to frustration. Research shows that people who eventually go on to lose their temper experience a successive build-up in emotion. Each check, insult, or act of rudeness leaves behind a residue of irritation. The state of edginess escalates until the 'last straw' reduces the individual to out-of-control rage. Unless the internal controls are slammed on quickly, this rage can turn to violence. The trick is not to let our frustration get the better of us.

Exercise

◆ Think about the last time you lost your temper.
◆ Can you recall how many irritating episodes led up to your loss of temper?
◆ How did you regain your self-control?
◆ Now think about a time when you *could* have become irritated but were able to control your frustration instead. How did you do that?

Studies of anger in the making show that it is the runaway critical and bitter thoughts that stoke up rage; changing these thoughts changes the emotion. To do this you can use a combination of techniques:

◆ Thought stopping
◆ Writing down thoughts
◆ Visualization (e.g. throwing negative ideas into a dustbin)
◆ Looking at the problem from another point of view (reframing)
◆ Empathizing for a moment with the other party. How was it they chose to do the things they did?
◆ Challenging perceptions:
  – Are they factual?
  – Are they exaggerated?
  – Are they logical?
  – Are they helpful?

Other techniques you might have thought of include: taking a walk, doing a breathing exercise, breaking off to do something pleasant and distracting, talking things over with a friend.

Channelling anger constructively

Anger is just as futile as fear. Typically it is based on blame. We blame others because they do not do the things we expect them to do. But they will choose to do the things that make most sense to them on the basis of the choices they know about and the information they have at the time. If they could do something better – given the situation – they would no doubt do it. However, once we get caught up in the blame game, anger follows as night follows day. The only thing we can do with it is find a constructive outlet for it. This could take the form of voicing one's concerns to the other person involved. To do that with emotional intelligence requires that we be clear about how their actions have hurt us or damaged other people.

Expressing anger has two negative consequences. First, anger feeds on anger. Research shows that people who blow their top are likely to do it again and again, getting more and more angry each time. This leads to chronic stress and to increased blood pressure with risks of strokes, heart disease and related illness. Secondly, expressing anger will alienate the people around you. Instead being persuaded to do something different, they will almost certainly stay out of your way. The best you will achieve is that they will learn to misbehave out of your sight. Meanwhile, the people who might take your side will be repelled by your lack of control and you will be less influential with them.

The marshmallow test

In a psychological experiment carried out in the 1960s, a group of four-year-olds underwent the 'marshmallow test'. The children were left in a room with a marshmallow each and told that if they could refrain from eating it until the experimenter came back they could have another one. They were left for 20 minutes – an eternity for some four-year-olds. About a third were unable to hold out and ate the sweet; the other two-thirds held on and received their reward of a second marshmallow. Those same four-year-olds were then tracked down 14 years later as they graduated from high school. It was found that the group able to delay gratification achieved test results far higher than the other group. More importantly, they scored higher for frustration tolerance, relationship skills, resilience under stress, and anger control. It was shown that impulse control was a far better predictor of academic success than IQ scores.

Impulse control

Fortunately, impulse control can be learned, although, for some, retraining may be hard. The effort is worth it because it is vital to conflict management as well as for long-term career success. In this section we review some techniques for emotional control.

If research shows that loss of temper results from a steady build-up of anger then, clearly, it is important to short-circuit the process before it spirals out of control. In order to do that we first need to recognize distress in the making. Being able to recognize anger or frustration and then interrupting the build-up is the key. People who do this take a walk, spend time by themselves, read, watch TV, listen to music, or practise a relaxation technique. Another useful tactic is to take the place of someone you know who is good at reacting to stress: what would that person say or do in your position?

A crucial factor in the escalation of emotion is internal self-talk. When crossed, we may engage in a stream of angry thoughts: blame, resentment or the 'I'll get you' response. To act effectively it is important to put the 'stop sign' on these thoughts and move quickly into a calmer frame of mind.

Exercise

◆ Recall an angry moment from your past. Fully relive the thoughts, emotions and behaviours you had at the time.
◆ Inside your own mind 'shout' STOP! Imagine a big red traffic 'STOP!' sign in your head.
◆ Now take a deep breath and breathe out all negative thoughts and emotions.
◆ Imagine yourself in a calmer, relaxed moment. 'Step inside' your body in that scenario and relive the very different thoughts, emotions and behaviours you had at the time.
◆ Do this several times if necessary.

Reframing problems

'Reframing' is the art of switching from one point of view to another. In general, useful points of view are broader, richer in information, disclose new ideas, and promote learning. By contrast, limited perspectives create a kind of tunnel vision which loops around the problem again and again, steadily ratcheting up the negative emotions. By exploring as many frames as we can for the problem, we enlarge our ability to deal with it.

Frames are used to look at a problem from different angles. Often disputes escalate because both parties are locked into their own position, refusing to see the other's. When both take the trouble to ask how the issue seems from a third party's point of view, or from the company's perspective, it enables them to step back from their own position and explore alternative solutions. A common method used by professional negotiators, when reaching agreement, is to use objective standards to decide on a fair deal. Thus buyers and sellers negotiating a property transfer might use fair market value for that type of property, as determined by a third party.

Using frames to resolve conflict

Penny was the manager of a team of consultants for a design agency. Most of the work involved creative projects for particular customers in marketing literature, advertising, presentation aids and corporate branding. All the members of her team except one were highly experienced designers and could be left to see a project through from start to finish while she was left to co-ordinate the work-flows and liaise with the customers. However, one of the team members – Joan – seemed impervious to coaching. Her projects nearly always over-ran budget and were usually late on delivery. As well as that the end-product frequently contained features that were at variance with the customer's expressed wishes, resulting in costly redesigns. Having had four meetings with Joan, Penny was at the end of her tether. The last meeting had ended on an acrimonious note with Joan accusing her of singling her out from the others and 'getting at her'. Even so, Penny called for what she felt might be their last meeting and to emphasize its importance booked the board-room for a half-day for the two of them.

On the day she decided to try a different approach. She put three goals up on the flip-chart:

◆ Meeting customer deadlines
◆ Keeping within budget
◆ Maintaining customer's approval

She asked Joan to look on the meeting as a brainstorming exercise just as if they were working on an advertising project together. First they would imagine a future in which all three goals were happening easily. What sort of people were they in that imaginary scene? Joan's first answer surprised her. She told her that she, Penny, would be 'around more' and would be far more precise in defining what she wanted from Joan. What was more, she would not have changed her mind once about the customer's wishes. This gave rise to a dialogue in which Penny discovered much about the way in which Joan perceived her. She, too, was able to open Joan's eyes to the way Penny saw her.

As well as the 'creative' frame, they explored several others with great success. In one frame Joan imagined one of her clients reacting with pleased surprise when an inspired portfolio arrived a week ahead of schedule. In another both Joan and Penny took a bird's-eye view of the agency and the impact their actions had on the team, the organization, and the industry in which they both worked. From this they realized that they still had much potential to explore and that there were untapped resources – people – they had still to call upon.

This meeting marked a turning point in their working relationship. Penny gave more thought to setting the parameters within which Joan would work and Joan responded by dramatically improving her ability to meet deadlines and manage her budgets.

How many frames did you notice in the story about Penny and Joan?

Your answers might have included:

♦ creativity frame
♦ future frame
♦ other people frame
♦ big picture frame
♦ solution frame.

Penny took positive action to prevent her mounting frustration from turning to unproductive anger. Using frames as a tool, she encouraged mutual collaboration and creativity in a way that meant she could side-step her personal position and explore many others. This interrupted her frustration and channelled the available energy into improved performance. She was also open and empathetic enough to hear about Joan's position and so discovered how she herself was contributing to the deadlock.

Creating a climate of openness

Exploring the perspectives of others – and of neutral parties – goes with developing a dialogue. Dialogue is key to defusing conflict and improving relationships. It is also linked to several useful interpersonal skills:

♦ defusing conflict
♦ developing relationships
♦ collaborating with others on a common goal
♦ influencing people.

Dialogue does not just mean exchanging views. It is the art, based on openness, of developing mutual understanding. In seeking this understanding it is not expected that you will *agree* with the other person's perspective. It may be enough just to respect the differences that exist between you or to understand how disagreement has become possible.

People who use dialogue seek to get behind fear: fear of being open, fear of being honest, fear of saying what one really thinks, fear of finding out what the other person really wants. In this sense, dialogue is emotionally intelligent insofar as it refuses to let negative emotions block effective communication.

To use dialogue, the first step is to be open about your feelings and needs. To do this it is important that you know what your feelings and needs in fact are. As we have seen, people who have developed the emotional intelligence to do this are often open to the feelings and needs of others. Thus an exchange takes place in which mutual solutions can be discussed openly, while recognizing differences.

Using dialogue

Consider this dialogue between Carl and Peter. Peter is Carl's manager and has called him in to discuss a staff problem. Notice how Peter uses Active listening to open up a dialogue.

> **Peter:** Carl – I want to talk to you about Emma. She's unhappy about the warning you've given her.

Carl: So she's come to you. I hope you told her where to go!

Peter: Well, actually, I agreed to talk to you about it. Carl, she's one of our best workers and I think we should be working hard to keep her here.

Carl: I also know that you appointed me the manager of this team and told me to make my own decisions. If you interfere now what message does that send to everybody here?

Peter: Well, I can see how it might look to you and I want you to know that whatever decision you make, I will support you on it. I'm not here to over-ride you. I just want to talk about the alternatives.

Carl: Well, I can't see any. Emma's been on my back since the day you promoted me. You know she wants the job for herself. She's continually stirring up trouble behind my back and I won't stand for it.

Peter: Your concern is that Emma won't let you manage the team, talks to others about your management, and talks to me about your decisions. Have I got that right?

Carl: Dead right.

Peter: I want to be straight with you. Emma's been with us for 12 years and she knows this business inside out. It would be hard to replace her. I don't want her to go. I also feel that if we can find some way to keep her in the team we are much more likely to meet our income targets.

Carl: Unless she changes her attitude – and that includes her not running to you every time I pull her up – I don't see how that's possible. In the long run the team will suffer – and results will go down anyway.

Peter: We agree that results, team performance and good management come first. What if we can get Emma to agree to that – do you think you could agree to withdraw your warning?

Carl: I'd need to see some evidence of a change of attitude first.

Peter: If you and Emma met and you told her what we'd talked about, and told her, too, that you will withdraw your warning if you see more cooperation from her over the next month, would you be happy with that?

Carl: I guess I'd be willing to give it a try.

Peter: Thank you. Your telling me that is a great weight off my mind. Will you let me know how it's working out in three weeks' time?

There are a number of helpful things Peter did to open up a dialogue with Carl. He was clear about his goals but balanced that with consideration for Carl's concerns. He confidently combined assertive speaking with flexibility.

It sometimes happens that agreements are not possible. If this is so, it is emotionally honest to accept that this is so without letting this fact harm your relationship with the other party. Peter searched for areas on which they could both agree and offered support for the decision Carl made. A crucial skill that he exercised was to separate the personal issues involved from the business ones. He therefore did not bring up the personality differences between Carl and Emma but focused on what was required for them to work together more effectively. He thus used a combination of emotionally intelligent moves. He avoided anger and fear, shared his worries, and imparted a sense of detachment which Carl was not slow to reciprocate.

How many bananas do you have?

Consider the answers to these questions:

- ◆ What must others never say about you?
- ◆ What triggers off anger in you? Why?
- ◆ What triggers off fear in you? Why?
- ◆ What triggers off despondency in you? Why?
- ◆ How do you most need others to treat you?

Answers to these questions may indicate those areas of your life where you feel threatened. They are what we call 'emotional bananas'. The idea for this comes from a common method used to catch monkeys in some remote areas in Asia. To catch a monkey the hunter will attach a small wicker basket to the floor of the jungle. The basket is constructed so that it is easy to put in a paw and take it out again provided the monkey is not holding anything. Then a banana or two is placed in the cage. The monkey sees this and grasps the banana. But, having seized the fruit, it won't let go. It is then easy prey for the hunter. Human beings are no different – we hold on to our emotional bananas for grim death because we feel threatened without them. Examples of emotional bananas include:

- Craving for status
- Demands for love or respect from others
- The need for control
- The cry for recognition
- Avoidance of discomfort.

The fewer bananas we carry around with us the less likely it is we will succumb to emotional hijacks. To reduce the power some of these bananas may have over us it is useful to substitute the word 'prefer' for 'must'. When we tell ourselves we must have something, we give away our power to it. When we tell ourselves 'Well, I would prefer if it others could give me X but I don't have to have it' we regain control over the banana.

Resolving differences

Emotionally intelligent people respect differences. They assume that no one person possesses the whole truth and that we have much to learn from each other. For this reason they are not emotionally defensive and do not get territorial with their ideas and skills. However, they are observant enough to realize that some people *are* defensive and they act diplomatically and with respect. At the same time, they do their best to break down barriers by being open and honest, and sharing their own beliefs and values.

Being sensitive to emotional 'musts' in others means we are in a position to help people regain control over them. The process through which we do this is simple:

- When differences come up, ask: 'If you had X, what would that do for you?'
- Listen carefully to the answer, reflect back concerns, and acknowledge the needs that emerge.
- Be equally frank about our own needs in return.
- Find a solution that satisfies all or part of both people's needs.

If no solution can be found – after careful, creative, mutual effort – acknowledge the differences that exist and move on to matters on which you can agree.

In summary ...

- **The key to managing conflicts with emotional intelligence is to disengage from negative emotion and replace this with cool reason.**

- **Disengage from fear and anger by taking constructive action and learning how to handle frustration.**

- **Cool down conflicts by exploring the perspectives through which other people are framing the situation. You can also use creative frames, goal frames and big picture frames to generate new solutions.**

◆ **Build dialogues with others through emotional honesty, openness and freedom from fear.**

◆ Watch out for your emotional bananas – areas in which you feel threatened – and learn to let them go.

◆ **Resolve differences by respecting other people's emotional bananas and finding out what lies behind their position.**

Chapter 6

Widening Your Influence

In this Chapter:

- ◆ **influencing others with integrity**
- ◆ **building up a network of allies and supporters**
- ◆ **making company politics work for you without playing games**
- ◆ **creating a good impression with senior people in your business.**

In this chapter, we describe how to keep your finger on your organization's pulse through networking and playing positive politics. We show you skills that enable you to influence people in your network, create a good impression and enter conversations with them easily. The key to all influence over the long term is integrity – staying true to your convictions. Integrity conveys itself in powerful ways: in your words, your gestures, your eyes and voice. If you combine this with trustworthy actions, you will build an emotional bank balance with your colleagues that you can call upon when you need help. Although it is possible to make short-term gains by flattery, playing games and acting opportunistically, in the long term you will make enemies and stir up distrust. You also run the risk that your supporters will be few.

When you are in trouble or need to exercise leadership, your potential supporters may look the other way.

The Caine Mutiny

The Caine Mutiny by Herman Wouk is a parable about leadership. The story is about the Second World War mutiny on the USS Caine. The commander's inflexibility imperilled his warship while on active service. When a typhoon blew up, Captain Queeg, who is overwhelmed by stress, insisted on obeying fleet orders issued hundreds of miles away rather than executing a turn of 180° to steer the ship away from the teeth of the raging storm and into safety. The more the wind blew, the more Captain Queeg insisted on holding to the course. In the end, the crew took command of the ship in order to save their lives. It was a mutiny, but their captain's intransigence left them with little choice. Naval discipline being what it is, the crew were given little chance of surviving the court-martial. But the trial showed up the crew's sincerity and their concern for the safety of the ship. Captain Queeg displayed only rigidity, intolerance and the principles of a martinet. The crew's actions were vindicated and it was their integrity that won out, while the credibility of Queeg – the emotionally unintelligent loner – was destroyed forever.

The winds that blow in communication may be for you, against you or at an angle to your chosen direction. Others' actions – like those of Queeg – are the 'winds' that blow in communication. Merely going with whatever wind is strongest at the time – the view of a senior manager, perhaps – is opportunism. Lacking integrity, the opportunist lacks credibility. Integrity comes from the inside, from strong values and clear goals. Emotionally intelligent people realize that their goals can only be achieved with and through others. Recognizing this, they develop the ability to negotiate so that mutual aims can be achieved. They will bend backwards to find common ground. But sometimes this is not possible, and like the crew of the USS Caine, we have to stand up for what we believe in. If we don't then sooner or later people will see through our essential phoniness. After all, those of us with emotional intelligence have the gift of distinguishing between trustworthy and insincere people.

Exercise

Think of a time when you were strong in expressing your beliefs and values.

◆ What did that feel like for you?
◆ What did others notice about you?
◆ What did you notice about yourself?

How can you take the strengths you displayed at this time and combine them with openness to the beliefs of others?

Where will you next demonstrate these combined qualities? With a customer? A friend? Someone senior to you? A family member? A salesperson?

Networking

Networking is an art. You may have learned to make and use social connections when you were young. Others have to develop the art. 'It is not what you know, but who you know' is an old maxim that remains true. Career advisors will tell you that the most effective way to secure another job is to network. More jobs are filled through contacts than are filled by advertising and headhunters. Successful entrepreneurs find markets for their ideas by networking. Managers with influence get to know a broad spectrum of people inside and outside their organizations. This puts them in touch with new ideas and potential allies. It gives them a wide circle of supporters to call upon when they want to get things done. They are always ready to give and take and think in advance of ways in which they could support people they meet. Knowing they have something to offer gives them the confidence to pick up the phone and suggest a meeting.

Getting started

But who should you contact? Your present friends, acquaintances and colleagues are the place to start. Although they may not be able to help you directly, they may know others who will be able to do so. It is said that you reach every person in the world if you meet seven people, who each in turn meet seven people and so on for a total of seven times.

Exercise

It helps to map your contacts on a large sheet of paper as described in this exercise.

◆ First decide on your goal. This could be starting a business, finding a job, influencing a decision, selling an idea, developing a new strategy, finding a financial backer, making a career move or achieving your annual goals.
◆ Now write down the names of everybody you know, no matter how brief your acquaintance.
◆ Mark in one colour the names of those who are closest to you personally.
◆ Mark in another colour the names of those who are likely to know others who can help you.
◆ Now highlight those on the list who are most likely to help you in achieving your goal.
◆ Start your contacts with those who may be of help, that are closest to you, and who are well connected.

Make sure that you get to know people in other departments. Attend company functions, get into conversations around the coffee machine, and sometimes stick around at the end of meetings to chat informally with people. Keep a record of those contacts you might want to meet again. Look out for opportunities to introduce people to others who may have interests in common. Set up informal groups so that people can meet together for a drink once a week – once others hear about groups like this they will want to be a part of them. If you set out three or four dates in advance it gives the group an identity that steadily grows stronger.

Alternatively, you can set up focus groups to discuss specific topics. Draw everyone into discussion of a subject to which they can all contribute. Be seen as a leader who is interested in people – seek them out and invite them to the occasions you have organized. If you don't have the opportunity to speak to them on the day, then call them afterwards: say you were sorry to miss them and invite them out for a drink. Above all, never overlook those junior to you. Today's newcomer might be tomorrow's senior manager. Besides, if you are only interested in people who can give you something now then you might as well not bother to network; others will soon see through the pretence.

Timing your entrance

A final key to networking is a sense of timing when entering conversations with others.

Getting Mum's attention

> Watching young children at a gathering of their mothers engrossed in conversation is instructive. From time to time, children approach the group to attract their mother's attention. Some children succeed, whilst others are ignored. What is the difference? The difference lies in the child's strategy. The children who interrupt their mothers successfully wait before talking. They watch their mothers and pick up the rhythm of the conversation. Then they intervene during a

lull. Those who intervene ineffectively, fail to
get the measure of the conversation, talk to
their mothers when the conversation is at its
height and are ignored. Some will then shout
or scream. This gets attention but not the
kind they want.

Entering a conversation with ease helps in networking and
in getting a hearing at meetings. People who are effective
at this, say at a professional gathering, observe a group of
strangers in conversation as they approach them. They
notice who is talking and who is listening. They decide
which of the people in the group they would feel
comfortable talking to and mirror their general demeanour
– degree of relaxation and general posture – and wait for a
while to take the temperature of the conversation. They
wait briefly for a lull and, as soon as an opportunity
presents itself, make a relevant comment to the chosen
person in the group or to the last person who spoke. They
go along with the group's conversation until they are
accepted before introducing a new subject. Supremely
confident people may use a full frontal attack by making a
joke or controversial statement as soon as they join a
group. If this is for you, then fine, but if you are not
supremely confident, a gentler approach may be easier.

Do not wait for too long before making a contribution in
a meeting. The longer you wait, the more reluctant you
are likely to be to say anything. If you are a new to a
meeting, sense the ebb and flow of the discussion, wait
for a subject to be aired on which you have a something
useful to say and, when there is a pause or a contributor

finishes speaking, make your contribution. If you find yourself waiting for too long for your subject to come up, ask an open question (one beginning with what, why, how, who, when or where) to clarify the goal of the discussion or the implications of a particular idea or suggestion.

Creating emotional bank balances

Your long-term aim must be to build up a network of supporters who can back you when you need help. They will be willing to do this if you have on deposit an emotional bank balance with each of them.

Exercise

◆ Take a good friend and imagine that you have a bank account divided into two halves with this person. On the left-hand side are the credits and on the right are the debits.

◆ Now recall all the things you have given your friend: favours, help, time, money, support, etc.

◆ Now recall all the things you have taken, including any liberties, arguments and unfriendly acts.

◆ How many items are on the left compared with the right? More importantly, how big are the credits compared with the debits?

These 'bank balances' are made up of help offered and given. Small acts include smiles, favours granted, a friendly word, kindness, the offer of a drink, advice, genuine interest in their personal problems, or an invitation. Larger ones might include job offers, loans, introductions, help, and forgiveness for a wrong.

Research shows that one of the distinguishing characteristics of people who are successful in their careers is that they have a wide network of contacts and supporters. When a job needs doing, or a problem needs to be solved, they are able to call on someone for help. They receive it because either they have a large credit at the bank or they are seen as influential people who may be able to help later on. Meanwhile the Captain Queegs of this world steadily grow more isolated while the ship sails on and leaves them behind.

Tip

Make it your practice to do at least one person a favour every day.

Which one will you do today? Do it now!

Playing politics

Many of us dislike politics. Yet it is a natural consequence of people working together in groups. Perhaps the 'politics' that people dislike is the self-serving kind. One of your authors worked in a company in which this kind of politics prevailed. Bad news was suppressed before it reached the Board as it might have reflected poorly on the divisional director. His managers colluded in this game. Lower down the ranks, the feeling was that there was little use in speaking up. The prevailing ethos was, 'If you scratch my back, I'll scratch yours'. This was politics of the negative kind: the self-serving manoeuvres of an in-group. But, properly speaking, politics means the setting of policy in everyone's interests. In groups, people naturally come together in order to decide on priorities, and on the allocation of resources for meeting them. People who are influential in politics are doing no more than advocating good arguments and getting support for their views. They are most likely to get a hearing if they argue for policies that benefit the largest number of people, or cater to the most important values.

Using power wisely

Constructive politics involves give and take. Using your connections is part of this. Sensing where the power lies is part of politics, as is identifying allies and minimizing resistance to your proposals. It can, however, have the best interests of colleagues and the company at heart. Networking is the next of kin to politics. Politics is using your network of contacts for a particular purpose, such as gaining acceptance for your ideas, resolving problems, completing a project, or furthering your career. Here are some tips that may help you to play politics usefully.

◆ When you are selling an idea that has implications beyond your direct responsibilities, think of the key players and decision-makers involved. Who are your supporters, who are the doubters and who are you unsure of?

◆ Talk informally to these people before you make a proposal.
  - Make sure that your assessment of your supporters is correct and that their needs are reflected in your ideas. Get commitment; ask them if they will support your ideas.
  - Probe to find out potential doubters' current thinking. If you are unsure which way they will sway, keep it in the back of your mind so that you are ready to respond if they oppose your proposal.
  - Predict as many of the doubters' objections as you can and pre-empt as many of them as possible.

◆ If the key decision-maker is not a supporter, then find out what is most important to him or her and adapt your plans to reflect these values.

◆ Use your informal networking skills to keep in touch with these people so that your finger is always on the pulse.

◆ Get the advice of senior people who can give you the bigger picture and the inside story on decisions and company plans. They can also give you insights about factions within the organization and the views of key players.

Give others support when they are in trouble, to ensure people are on your side when the chips are down. Who knows, a person who needs support now may be your boss someday. Make sure you respect people's position in the hierarchy. Even in laid-back companies it is easy to offend a person if you go above them without prior consultation.

Give the person concerned a fair chance to sort out a problem they are causing before going to their boss.

Become an observer of organizational politics. Notice who holds most sway in meetings. It is not always the most senior person. It may be the one with the greatest expertise, best connections, or most charisma.

Creating an impression

First impressions count. Although other impressions count too, there is no doubt that it helps if others perceive you to be credible from the start. Creating the right impression starts on the inside with how you feel about yourself and the message that you want to put across. It is likely that the impression you make on others is partly determined by your own self-image.

How belief affects experience

> Francis Galton, who initiated the science of heredity and revealed the individuality of fingerprints, vividly illustrated the power of thinking on people's response to us. In an act of self-hypnosis, he imagined himself to be loathsome. Then he set off on a walk through the streets of London. People abused him without provocation; he was manhandled by a docker and kicked by a horse.

Such is the power of thinking over people's reactions to you. Positive thinking leads to a positive response;

negative thinking to a negative response. The first step in positive thinking is to relax. It is difficult to think constructively if you are tense. One of these ways of relaxing may suit you.

◆ Take a short stroll and let the easy movement of your body relax you.
◆ Take ten easy, deep breaths in a quiet spot.
◆ Think of a time, perhaps on holiday, when you were at ease with yourself and the world around you.
◆ Locate the source of tension in your body, then imagine it having a particular size, shape, weight and colour. Imagine the size of the area gradually changing and its colour fading and as it does so the weight will reduce. Eventually, you will find that the shape disappears and with it your tension.
◆ Take a moment to relax yourself from head to toe. Start with your toes, relax these and then let the muscles relax in the rest of your foot. Gradually move up your body, to the muscles of your legs, torso, neck and head. Take your time and be specific; relax all the muscles of your body. You can learn to do this in a minute or less.

Once you are relaxed, think positively about what you want to achieve in an upcoming communication. Here is a reminder of some of the techniques we covered in Chapter 2.

◆ Mentally rehearse the positive goal that you want to achieve. Make it vivid. Imagine what you will see, hear and feel when you have achieved the goal.

- ◆ Think of times in the past that you have handled challenges successfully, remember those feelings and your goal at the same time.
- ◆ Run through your own strengths and how they will support you in achieving the goal.

Making the first meeting count

Although the journey starts on the inside, it does not end there. To create an impression, step into the shoes of your audience and predict their values. Rehearse an upcoming meeting and think how you will respond to awkward questions and difficulties that might arise. Dress the part and communicate in a style that will exert the influence that you want.

Creating a good first impression

> Already a successful operational line manager, Jane felt that she was ready for promotion to the MD's position that was due to fall vacant. Jeans and t-shirt were the order of the day in the co-operative in which she worked. People dressed casually, indeed some would say scruffily. The co-operative was highly successful. It had attracted venture capital to enable it to expand rapidly and was in negotiation with another venture capitalist for further funding. Unlike many of her colleagues, Jane guessed rightly that the new venture capitalist would be formal in his attitudes to dress. Before meeting him, she

made subtle adjustments in her appearance and demeanour. She wore trousers instead of jeans and a shirt rather than a t-shirt. She rehearsed what she would say and questions she could ask. She predicted the venture capitalist's values and the awkward questions he might throw at her. It enabled her to be confident and sure in her communication with the venture capitalist. His opinion held sway in deciding who would be the next managing director. Fortunately, he saw Jane as a credible manager of stature and supported her application for the vacant MD position.

Jane was astute enough to work on her first impressions. She was able to be flexible because she was secure enough in her own self-worth to realise that her clothes were a minor issue compared to her aspirations. Sacrificing her preferred dress style, she concentrated on winning an ally who would help her achieve her long-term aim. Her strong self-image provided a platform for success. She had some good ideas and had thought through her plans. She was ready to deal with criticisms and demonstrate her readiness for the role to which she aspired.

Interacting with seniors

We have spent many years in working to develop people in business, both as managers ourselves, and as trainers and coaches. In the course of business we often hear moans about the actions of seniors: that their decisions make no sense, that they are out of touch, secretive and arbitrary. Yet we are continually struck by the fact that, when it is the turn of the moaners to be promoted, they act in the very same way that they complained of when they were juniors.

Senior managers and directors are just as human as the rest of us. They grapple with insoluble problems, undergo crises of self-doubt, sometimes question their careers, or their fitness for the job, and have to balance these difficulties with their personal worries. Added to this, they have to put up with the burdens of responsibility that go with seniority. This can be a lonely place to be. The first step in widening your influence with those senior to you is to treat them as human beings like yourself. First, you will need to distinguish between the person and the role. The person is one just like yourself; the role involves leadership (although not all senior managers exercise this successfully). To interact with emotional intelligence you will need to combine personal relationship skills with organizational awareness.

In an organization, leaders are provided with formal authority through which they are expected to exercise a vision of the organization's success. This means taking the long view and focusing on the big picture rather than detail. It also means that they have to rely on subordinates to carry through the day-to-day work – even though they are still responsible when things go wrong. A common frustration for senior managers is to be confronted with details about problems they know little about. That is why they place great value on people who show loyalty and can be relied upon to come up with solutions rather than problems.

The attitudes to adopt

To interact successfully with seniors you will therefore need to demonstrate certain characteristics to them:

- respect for the burdens of office (you don't necessarily have to respect the person)
- loyalty to the team/organization/company leadership
- reliability in managing day-to-day difficulties
- an appreciation of the big picture
- a proactive, solution-focused approach
- decisiveness and the ability to back decisions with facts and logic.

The next time you present your ideas to a senior manager or director, use the following questions to guide your presentation:

- Have I earned the trust of the other party? If not, how can I earn it?
- Have I selected a time and place that enables this person to give me a fair hearing?
- Have I put together a proposal that is as brief as possible?
- Have I linked the proposal to positive consequences for the organization or division?
- Does my proposal fit with organizational strategies?
- Will my proposal enable the senior manager to shine in front of their colleagues?
- Is my proposal factual, well-researched, and based on clearly written premises?
- Have I considered the pitfalls, costs and impact on customers and other teams?

Despite your best efforts you may meet with objections. Treat these not as a comment on your work but on the senior manager's concerns. They may be privy to information that you do not have. Or they may be dealing with organizational politics – the concerns of their seniors and colleagues. If, in spite of everything, your major ideas are rejected, then do what you can to salvage the ones that are acceptable. If you have to withdraw, then do so quietly and fight on another day. At least you will have earned respect for your positive approach.

In summary ...

◆ **Always act with integrity and stand up for what you believe in. People will eventually see through phoniness and opportunism.**

◆ **Successful people nearly always have a large network of contacts, allies and supporters.**

◆ **Build up your contacts through your current network of friends and colleagues, taking opportunities that come your way, and setting up informal groups.**

◆ **Be sure to exercise tact when timing your entrance into a new group.**

◆ Create emotional bank balances in your favour with as many people as you can. They will become your allies when you need them.

◆ Use constructive politics to get acceptance for your ideas by calling on your allies and canvassing the support of seniors.

◆ You can influence seniors through poise and confidence, being clear about your goals, and adapting your proposals to the needs of the organization.

◆ When talking with seniors, pitch your ideas so that they take into account the responsibilities they have at heart.

About the Authors

John Eaton PhD and Roy Johnson MBA are the Managing Partners of Coaching Solutions, an organization which coaches directors and managers in some of Britain's best-known corporations. Their training seminars have created innovations in the fields of coaching, emotional intelligence, dialogue communication and leadership (see www.coachingsolutions.co.uk). They also offer web-based coaching and training through their innovative on-line service, coachskills.com

John started business life as a financial analyst with Dun & Bradstreet and then with Chemical Bank before becoming a senior manager with EXFINCO. His experience in management taught him that if managers knew what they were doing they rarely stayed around long enough to teach others what they knew. John received his doctorate in Psychology from the University of Lancaster in 1998 for his research into interpersonal communication. This taught him absolutely nothing about emotional intelligence other than the fact that most psychologists don't have any.

Roy is also Director of Pace, an award-winning training company, which has trained and coached managers in blue-chip organisations throughout the UK. Before founding Pace, he was a senior executive in Rank Xerox, experiencing the pleasures and pains of managing and negotiating with people from diverse cultures. Looking back at his first career step into the Royal Navy, he can see how greater emotional intelligence would have sustained him in its formal, hierarchical organization.

Roy and John have made good use of their ability to sit on the sidelines and watch others manage. They are also the authors of numerous published articles as well as *Training with NLP* (Gower), *Business Applications of NLP* (Gower) and *Coaching Successfully* (Dorling Kindersley).

You can contact John and Roy at Coaching Solutions, PO Box 42, Watlington SPDO, Oxfordshire OX9 5XU Tel: (01491) 614833/613956.
Email: info@coachingsolutions.co.uk

Further Reading from How To Books

2-4-6-8 How Do You Communicate?, Phillip Khan-Panni, 2001.

A to Z of Correct English, Angela Burt, 2000.

Blank Page to First Draft in 15 Minutes, Phillip Khan-Panni, 2001.

How to Talk to the Media, Judith Byrne, 2000.

Increase Your Word Power, Angela Burt, 2001.

Making an After Dinner Speech, John Bowden, 2nd edition, 2001.

Making Great Presentations, Ghassan Hasbani, 1999.

Say it with Pictures, Dr Harry Alder, 2001.

Toasts & Short Speeches, John Bowden, 2000.

Writing, Speaking, Listening, Helen Wilkie, 2001.

**For comprehensive information on How To Books'
titles visit How To Books on-line at
www.howtobooks.co.uk**